SOUPER BOWL
OF RECIPES

Nan Perry
Betty Arnsparger
Nancy Siebert
Dorothy Shula

Northwoods Press, Inc.

PO Box 249

Stafford, Va. 22554

USA

ISBN 0-89002-188-0, Paperback
ISBN 0-89002-189-9, Cloth

Library of Congress Catalog Card Number 80-82260

NORTHWOODS PRESS, INC.
PO BOX 249
STAFFORD, VA 22554 USA

FORWORD

To the beginning cooks and the experts; to the collectors of cookbooks; to the gift givers; and to football fans across the country, this book is dedicated.

The true friendship between four close friends made the idea of this book an exciting project and challenge for us all.

The wonderful co-operation and interest shown by the many contributors from East Coast to West Coast who were contacted, made the preparation of this book pure joy. They have not only shared their favorite recipes, but their personal remarks which will show the true meaning of a good sport—the willingness and generosity to share with others.

We are grateful for their time and for their participation.

P erry, Nan
A rnsparger, Betty Jane
S iebert, Nancy
S hula, Dorothy

Our appreciation for cover design and interior art goes to Sister Carol Ann, Villa Maria Convent, Bernardine Sisters O.S.S., Stamford, Conn.

DEDICATION TO CONTRIBUTORS:

This book is dedicated to the twenty eight National Football teams across the nation, and to the many fans who support them.

To the players, coaches, coaching staffs, owners, and managers; to the famous and maybe not so famous, to the alumni, we give our sincere thanks and appreciation.

Without their participation and willingness to share, this book would not have been possible.

We certainly hope the pleasure you receive from this great collection of recipes and information pertinent to each person, will be as great as the pleasure it has been for us in preparing it.

In presenting this book of recipes to the public, there has been no attempt to give a complete cookbook. This is simply a collection of favorite recipes from the members, past and present, of the National Football League.

P erry, Nan
A rnsparger, Betty Jane
S iebert, Nancy
S hula, Dorothy

TABLE OF CONTENTS

P.A.S.S.
the
Appetizers and
Hors D'Oeuvres

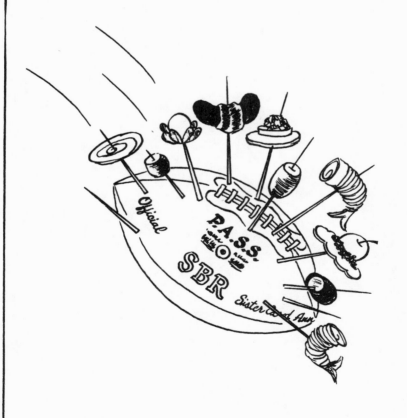

San Diego Chargers
37 Fullback

HANK BAUER

DEEP FRIED WON TONS

2 lbs. ground beef
1 garlic bud
2—4 T. soy sauce
1 ginger root
1 bunch small green onions

peanut oil
1—2 packages (frozen) won ton skins
salt and pepper
½ head lettuce

Mix in a large bowl the burger, soy sauce, finely diced bunch of onions, finely diced half head of lettuce, finely grated garlic bud—½ to a whole depending on taste, finely grated ginger root and salt and pepper. Add amounts of soy sauce, ginger root and garlic until it smells according to your taste. Add 1 tablespoon of salt & pepper and mix thoroughly using both hands in a squeezing fashion. Lay out a number of skins and put a heaping tablespoon of the meat on each one. Wet two edges of the square skin and pinch together forming a triangle. It is similar to a small egg roll. After preparing all the won tons, heat the peanut oil and deep fry. NOTE: *The taste will vary depending on your seasoning—even a lightly seasoned fried won ton makes a good party treat or side dish.*

•   •   •

Philadelphia Eagles
72 Guard

WADE KEY

CHILE CON QUESO

2 lb. velveeta cheese
1 can rotel tomatoes
1 jalapeno pepper—fine chopped
½—lb. longhorn cheese

Melt chunked velveeta cheese with tomatoes. Add pepper *only* if you desire spiced foods. Grate cheese and stir in until thick. Serve in dish that can be kept warm. Good with doritos.

STEVE YOUNG

New York Giants
74 Offensive Tackle

APPLESAUCE MEATBALLS

This recipe comes from my German grandmother. We've given it to lots of friends and it's very popular.

2 lbs. ground beef	½ cup applesauce
¼ cup bread or cracker crumbs	¼ teas. pepper
¼ cup chopped onions	½ teas. garlic salt
1 egg	dash nutmeg

Mix all ingredients. Form into balls. Roll balls in flour. Brown on all sides in oil. In fry pan, electric oven or crockpot put 2½–3 cups catsup and ¼ cup water (enough for meatballs to simmer in and be partially covered). Simmer meatballs in sauce slowly for at least 1 hour—longer if possible. Good to make ahead—refrigerate and warm up later.

•   •   •

DR. DANIEL FORTMANN

Hall of Fame
Chicago Bears
21 Guard, Linebacker

BAKED PAPAYA MAUNA KEA

Mauna Kea Hotel serves this as an appetizer. We use it at brunch, lunch or dinner as a salad. We also leave out the melted butter and serve cold without baking. For low cal, use mostly cottage cheese, not as yummy, but one's conscience feels better. Mary.

3 papayas, halved & seeded	1½ cups cottage cheese
1½ cups cream cheese	1 teas. curry powder
2 T. white raisins	½ cup thinly sliced water chestnuts
2 T. chopped chutney	

Mix and fill papayas with cheeses, curry, raisins, water chestnuts, and chutney. Sprinkle with ¼ cup cinnamon-sugar and ¼ cup of melted butter. Bake at 450° for 15 minutes. Can be prepared ahead, refrigerate and bake for serving.

Atlanta Falcons
79 Defensive End

JEFF YEATES

CRABMEAT HORS D'OEUVRE

one 7 oz. can white crab meat
1 small jar cheese whiz (soft)
1 stick butter (soft)
3 T. mayonnaise

½ teas. seasoned salt
½ teas. garlic salt
6 English muffins

Mix above all together—cut English muffins in half. Spread ingredients on muffins and place on cookie sheet—freeze for at least two hours. Take from freezer and put in broiler for 5 minutes. Cut muffins into 4 pieces. (tastes great and super to make ahead of time!)

● ● ●

Miami Dolphins
73 Defensive Lineman

BOB BAUMHOWER

CRABMEAT COCKTAIL

Serves 4

12 oz. Alaskan king crab meat
½ oz. lemon juice
3 oz. mayonnaise
salt and pepper to your taste

Mix well together. Fill ½ peeled avocado with mixture. Place on large lettuce leaf on a bed of finely crushed ice. Serve with the following sauce:

1 C. catsup
½ C. chili sauce
1 T. vinegar
1 teas. worcestershire sauce

1 teas. horseradish
¼ teas. celery salt
¼ teas. tabasco sauce
juice of 1 lemon

Mix well and chill.

TEX SCHRAMM

Dallas Cowboys
President

ARTICHOKE NIBBLES

Great as an hors d'oeuvre. I have also served these squares with a big salad instead of bread or rolls. A favorite of our family. Marty.

2—6 oz. jars marinated artichoke hearts   1/8 teas. pepper
1 large onion finely chopped   1/8 teas. oregano
1 garlic clove minced   1/8 teas. tabasco sauce
4 eggs   ½ lb. grated cheddar cheese
¼ cup fine dry seasoned bread crumbs   2 T. minced parsley
½ teas. salt

Drain marinade from 1 jar artichokes into skillet. Drain other jar of artichokes discarding marinade. Chop artichokes and set aside. Saute onion, garlic in marinade in skillet until onion is limp, about five minutes. Beat eggs until fluffy then add bread crumbs, salt, pepper, oregano and tabasco sauce. Stir in cheese, parsley, artichokes and onion mixture. Mix well and pour into a greased 11x17 inch baking pan. Bake in a preheated 325° oven 30 minutes. Let cool in pan and cut in 1 inch squares. Serve warm or cold. Makes about 6 dozen. These can be frozen and then reheated in oven 10—12 minutes.

• • •

JOHN NORTH

Atlanta Falcons
Backfield Coach

ARTICHOKE SPREAD

1 large can artichoke hearts
1 cup mayonnaise
1 cup parmesan cheese

Drain artichoke hearts, get all water out, use paper towel to pat if necessary. Chop up or shred just before ready to serve. Mix the three ingredients and cook in casserole about 30 minutes until browned. Spread on Melba toast rounds.

Pittsburgh Steelers
Vice President

ART ROONEY, JR.

CHEESEBALL

2—8 oz. cream cheese (Phila)
1 sm. (8½ oz.) can crushed pineapple (drained)
1 green pepper (chopped finely)
1 T. onions (chopped finely)
1 T. seasoned salt (Lawry's)
2 cups nuts (chopped pecans)

Mix all but 1 cup nuts together with fork. Form ball with hands. Roll into nuts (other 1 cup nuts). NOTE: *Wash hands before rolling into other 1 cup nuts.*

* * *

Philadelphia Eagles
Assistant Coach,
Defensive Backs

FRED BRUNEY

CRAB MOUSSE

Serve with varied assortment of crackers.

Let stand:

2 small packages Knox gelatin (2T.) dissolved in ¼ cup hot water.

Heat in pan:

1—8 oz. package cream cheese
1 sm. grated onion
1 can cream of mushroom soup (undiluted)

Mix all together with 2 packages frozen or canned crab meat, 1 cup finely chopped celery, 1 cup Hellman's mayonnaise, and pour into pretty mold. Refrigerate til serving time.

BOB GRIESE
Miami Dolphins
12 Quarterback

CUBAN SANDWICHES

Take 1 loaf of Cuban bread and slice in half lengthwise. Remove dough. Spread mayonnaise on one half; mustard on the other. Lay in a generous supply of thinly sliced Cuban ham topped with sliced, sweet pickles. Next a layer of thinly sliced Cuban pork (this pork is very spicey and should be used in small quantities). Sprinkle chopped, sweet onion over the pork. Add thinly sliced swiss cheese and put lid on sandwich. Brush melted butter on both sides of Cuban bread and grill until cheese is melted and bread loaf is mildly toasted. Slice loaf on angles for easier eating. One loaf should make 6—7 small sandwiches.

• • •

DERREL LUCE
Baltimore Colts
58 Linebacker

SAUSAGE PINWHEELS

APPETIZER: OVEN: 375°

1 can store bought biscuits, 1 pound pork sausage (hot). Press together biscuit dough, then roll out thinly. Spread sausage evenly over dough: roll up as a jelly roll; wrap in waxed paper: chill or freeze for several hours. When ready to serve, slice thin and bake on ungreased cookie sheet 15 minutes until brown. Serve very hot. Serves 15.

• • •

MICHAEL (MO) SCARRY
Miami Dolphins
Defensive Line Coach

MO'S "STUFF" ON FRENCH BREAD

Brown 2 lb. ground beef, seasoned with a little Lawry's season salt. Cut 1 loaf french bread in half lengthwise. Spread each half evenly with soft oleo. Spread meat, sliced onions and mushrooms (either or both). Pour ketchup over all. (Barbecue sauce may be used instead of ketchup for a different flavor). Alternate slices of various cheeses (American, Swiss, Provolone, Cheddar) on top of all. Place in 350° oven until cheese melts. Slice in desired size pieces and eat like pizza.

Hall of Fame
Green Bay
Washington
Coach

IN MEMORY OF
VINCENT T. LOMBARDI

CHICKEN LIVER PATE'

Boil 1 lb. chicken livers in water, barely covering for 15 to 20 minutes. Drain and place hot livers in blender. Add:

2 teas. salt
pinch cayenne
1 cup butter
1/2 teas. nutmeg

2 teas. dry mustard
1/4 teas. ground cloves
1/4 cup minced onions

Mold. Serve with crackers.

•   •   •

Tampa Bay Buccaneers
62 Guard-Tackle

JEFF WINANS

BEAN DIP

Goes well with any combination of mexican dinner.

2 cans of favorite chili (Hormel extra hot)
    Stir together with
1-8 oz. package of Philadelphia cream cheese
    At medium heat. Stirring frequently to mix up cream cheese,   then add:
2—3 cups shredded American medium cheese
    Stir until it's mixed together with cream cheese and beans. Then

1 cup of onions mixed in after everything is mixed together well and the bean dip is just about to boil. Add your favorite brand of hot sauce to liken with your own taste buds. Stir one final time and pour into bowls and ready to eat. May be frozen and reheated. *If you like cheese, the bean dip really is good with a few drinks before a nice Mexican or Spanish dinner.*

JOHN SYMANK

Baltimore Colts
Defensive Backfield Coach

BLACK-EYED PEA DIP

Chop:

1/2 bell pepper
8 jalapeno peppers (minus seeds)

2 stalks celery
1 large onion

Add:

1 teas. pepper
1/2 cup catsup
1 T. salt
3 chicken bouillon cubes

1/4 teas. nutmeg
1/4 teas. cinnamon
1 teas. tabasco (or more)

Bring above to boil and simmer 10 minutes. Then add:

2 cans or about 4—5 cups (cooked) black-eyed peas
2 cups canned tomatoes
1 teas. garlic salt

Cook for 30 minutes. Blend 1/2 cup bacon drippings and 3 T. flour and add to above to thicken. Serve with corn chips.

•   •   •

VINCE PAPALE

Philadelphia Eagles
83 Wide Receiver

BLUE CHEESE COLD VEGETABLE DIP

1 small cup up white onion
1 cup mayonnaise
1/3 cup vegetable oil
1/4 cup ketchup
2 teas. sugar
2 teas. vinegar

1 teas. prepared mustard
1/2 teas. salt
1/2 teas. paprika
1/4 teas. celery salt
dash pepper
4 oz. pkg. crumbled blue cheese
(Save some for garnish)

Put all ingredients in a blender except cheese and blend until smooth. Remove, stir in cheese, cover and chill. Garnish with leftover cheese.

Philadelphia Eagles
55 Inside Linebacker

FRANK LeMASTER

CHIPPED BEEF DIP (HOT)

1-8 oz. pkg. cream cheese
8 oz. sour cream
1 small jar chipped beef
2 T. milk
½ teas. garlic salt

½ teas. pepper
½ teas. salt
1 T. butter
1 pkg. pecan halves

Combine cream cheese, sour cream, chipped beef, garlic salt, milk and pepper. Place in shallow pyrex dish. Next: Brown pecans in butter and salt. Then pour them over the above mixture. Heat for 20 minutes at 350°. Serve with Taco chips.

• • •

Baltimore Colts
President and Owner

ROBERT IRSAY

CRAB CURRY DIP

This is a favorite of our guests. Could be used with potato chips, various crackers or cut up fresh vegetables like carrots, celery, mushrooms, etc. Harriet.

⅓ cup mayonnaise
8 oz. package cream cheese
6 oz. crab meat (frozen or canned)
1 teas. curry powder
1 T. grated onion
1 teas. lemon juice (fresh)
¼ teas. salt

If making in advance, add crab meat just before serving.

BLANTON COLLIER

Cleveland Browns
Alumni Browns
Head Coach

CURRY DIP

I like it especially with raw vegetables.

1 cup Hellman's mayonnaise
3 T. catsup
3 teas. curry powder
1 T. worcestershire sauce
1 T. grated onion
dash garlic juice
salt and pepper to taste

Mix and store in refrigerator.

•   •   •

VERN DEN HERDER

Miami Dolphins
83 Defensive End

DEVILED DIP

Great with chips.

1-5 oz. jar pimento cheese spread
1-2¼ oz. can deviled ham
½ cup mayonnaise or salad dressing
2 T. minced parsley
1 T. minced onion
dash msg
4 drops tabasco sauce

Mix together with electric mixer.

Pittsburgh Steelers
66 Offensive Tackle

TED PETERSEN

DILL DIP

Great for Social Gatherings!

> *1 cup Miracle Whip salad dressing*
> *1 cup sour cream*
> *2 T. minced onion*
> *2 T. beau mond seasoning*
> *2 T. dill weed*

Mix and refrigerate.

•　　•　　•

New Orleans Saints
1 Placekicker

GARO YEPREMIAN

HUMMOS (CHICK-PEA DIP)

> *1 can chick peas (17 oz. can)　1 cup taheen (sesame seed oil)*
> *2 cloves garlic　　(can be bought at Middle East store)*
> *¾ teas. salt　　　　　　　　　　　　　　olive oil*
> *¾ cup lemon juice　　　　　　　　　　　　paprika*
> *　　　　　　　　　　　　　　　　chopped parsley*

Pour the contents of the can of chick peas with its liquid into a blender. Turn the blender on (puree) until the chick peas are mashed. Add the garlic, salt and lemon juice and blend again. Finally add the taheen and turn the blender on again for a couple of seconds. Turn out the hummos into a wide shallow bowl. Sprinkle the top of the hummos lightly with olive oil, paprika and chopped parsley. Serve with pita bread or potato chips for dipping. 10 servings.

DAN ALEXANDER

New York Jets
60 Offensive Guard

LOUISIANA CRAYFISH DIP

Although this is considered a dip, to be eaten with melba rounds, it is delicious
served on rice and will generously serve 5 people.

3 lbs. peeled crayfish tails	*1 teas. black ground pepper*
⅔ C. oil	*1 T. red cayenne pepper,*
1 stick oleo	*ground (add to suite taste)*
2 C. green onions, chopped	*2 T. parsley flakes*
(both green and white parts)	*4—6 oz. can drain most water off*
4 pieces sliced garlic	*1½ cans Campbells*
1 can mushrooms	*cream of mushroom soup*
(stems & pieces)	*(do not dilute)*

Saute green onions in ½ stick oleo and ¼ cup cooking oil, until limp and
start to turn darker. Add garlic, black and red pepper, parsley flakes and
mushrooms. Cook 5 minutes and then add soup. Continue cooking 5 more
minutes. In meantime, fry crayfish tails in ½ stick oleo and remaining oil,
turning until the crayfish change to a salmon color and form a crust on bottom of pan. Remove from fire and add to other mixture, scraping crust off
bottom of pan. Continue cooking for about 15 more minutes, on low fire,
stirring occasionally to keep from sticking.

• • •

JOHN MEYER

Green Bay Packers
Linebacker Coach

GRAB BAG VEGETABLE DIP

½ cup sour cream	*2 teas. dry mustard*
2 cups mayonnaise	*½ teas. salt*
½ teas. Accent	*1 teas. lemon juice (fresh)*
¼ cup horseradish (mild)	

Mix the above together and dip fresh vegetables:

raw fresh mushrooms	*cherry tomatoes*
raw zucchini	*avacado*
artichoke hearts	*raw cauliflower*
hearts of palm	

Souper Bowl of Recipes—12

Philadelphia Eagles
69 Guard

WOODY PEOPLES

KRUGER BEAN DIP

1 large cream cheese
1 large can bean dip
20 drops tabasco
1 small carton sour cream
1 pkg. taco mix
1 bunch green onions

Mix together in mixer; top with lots of grated cheddar cheese. Bake at 350°
for 30 minutes or until very hot. Serves 8.

* * *

Green Bay Packers
10 Quarterback

LYNN DICKEY

MEXICAN DIP

1 8 oz. can tomatoes & green chilies
1 onion chopped
1 clove garlic, finely chopped
1 lb. velveeta cheese (cubed)
1 teas. worcestershire sauce
1 teas. tabasco sauce
1 teas. chili powder

Saute onion and garlic in 2 T. of butter. Reserve 2 T. liquid from tomato and
green chili sauce and blend 1 T. of flour with it. Add tomatoes and green
chili sauce to onion and garlic and bring to a boil. Add cheese and mix til
melted. Add thickening and seasoning. Stir til thick over moderate heat.
Serve hot or cold with Doritos chips.

KEVIN McLAIN

Los Angeles Rams
50 Linebacker

MEXICAN CHEESE DIP

1 lb. hamburger
small diced onion
1 pkg. taco seasoning mix
8 oz. velveeta cheese
small can diced green chilies
1 can chili beans
Doritos
*Vary amounts according to desired quantity and personal taste.

In frying pan, brown hamburger, add onion, mixing about half of taco seasoning mix. Remove from heat. In pan melt cheese, add green chilies, chili beans, hamburger mixture and remainder of taco seasoning. Mix well, heat thoroughly. Serve as a dip with Doritos or spread chips on cookie sheet and pour mixture over chips.

* * *

MARK MURPHY

Washington Redskins
29 Safety

MURPHY's MEXICAN DIP

1 can taco sauce
¾ lb. Monteray Jack cheese
1 whole tomato
1 whole green pepper
2 T. diced onion

Place taco sauce in pan on low heat. Dice up the tomato and peppers. Cut the cheese up into large chunky pieces. Add the diced tomato, pepper, and onion and the cheese to the taco sauce. Continue to cook at low heat, stirring the mixture until the cheese has melted. Keep the dip over low heat while consuming dip. Dip is best with Dorito chips.

Los Angeles Rams
11 Quarterback

PAT HADEN

PECAN DIP

1 8 oz. pkg. softened cream cheese
2 T. milk
1 2½ oz. jar sliced dried beef
1 teas. onion salt
1 cup sour cream

Combine all ingredients and spoon into small casserole. Heat and crisp ½ cup chopped pecans in 2 T. butter. Sprinkle over cheese mixture. Bake at 350° for 20 minutes uncovered. Serves 12—15.

• • •

Buffalo Bills
Assistant Coach

WILLIE ZAPALAC

SPINICH DIP

Thaw and drain 1 pkg. of frozen chopped spinach. Press all water out. Add:

¾ cup cottage cheese
¾ cup sour cream
½ cup mayonnaise
½ cup dried parsley
4 scallions, chopped
dash tabasco, worchestershire, garlic and seasoned salt

Serve with Prontos, Fritos or crackers.

RON McCARTNEY

Atlanta Falcons
56 Linebacker

VEGETABLE DIP

1 cup sour cream
1 cup mayonnaise
1 heaping teas. dill flakes

1/2 teas. celery salt
1 heaping teas. parsley flakes
1 teas. minced onion

Mix together and refrigerate at least one hour before serving.

* * *

ARCHIE MANNING

New Orleans Saints
8 Quarterback

WATER CHESTNUT DIP

1 8 oz. carton sour cream
1 cup Hellman's mayonnaise
1 8 oz. can water chestnuts
drained & chopped

2 T. soy sauce
1/2 cup chopped parsley
3 green onions, chopped
2—3 drops tabasco

Mix ingredients well and serve as a dip. Makes 3 cups dip.

* * *

GREG BREZINA

Atlanta Falcons
50 Linebacker

YOGURT DIP

1/2 cup plain yogurt
1/2 cup mayonnaise
1 T. onion flakes

1 teas. poppy seed
salt to taste
1 teas. spike seasoning (found mostly
in health food stores)

Mix all ingredients together and keep refrigerated. Serve with raw vegetables.

Minnesota Vikings
73 Right Tackle (Offense)

RON YARY

EGG ROLLS

Preparation: brown 1 lb. ground pork (you may substitute shredded chicken or shrimp). Prepare filling: Blanch 3 lbs. of bean sprouts in hot water; drain.

1 cup of finely sliced bamboo shoots;
1 cup of finely chopped celery;
1 cup of chopped water chestnuts;

Add ground pork and mix well. Season with salt, black pepper, and 1 teas. of accent.

Skins: Use above filling to fill prepared egg roll skins. Roll. Turn in ends of skins. Use egg to seal ends of egg rolls. Deep fry until brown. Drain on paper towel to remove excess grease. Cut into three segments before serving.

•   •   •

Miami Dolphins
Defensive Backfield Coach

TOM KEANE

"HOT" CHEESE SQUARES

1 lb. cheddar cheese, grated
1 lb. Monterey Jack cheese, grated
2—4 jalapeno peppers, chopped fine
6 eggs, beaten lightly
⅔ cup pet milk

Mix cheeses and put ½ into 9x13 pan. Spread chopped pepper over cheese, then top with remaining cheese. Mix eggs and pet milk and pour over cheese. Bake at 350° for 35—40 minutes. Cut into 1 inch squares and serve hot or cold. Hot is better!

ED O'NEIL

Detroit Lions
55 Middle Linebacker

ITALIAN SAUSAGE COCKTAIL SQUARES

Very tasty hors d' oeuvre.

1 cup grated mozzarella cheese
2 lbs. Italian sausage (sweet & hot)
3 tubes of crescent rolls (Pillsbury refrigerated)
1 cup romano cheese
1 cup parmesan cheese
5 eggs or (4 if extra large)

Preheat oven to 350⁰. Spread and pat 1½ tubes of crescent roll dough on bottom of 9x13 glass baking dish. Brown sausage (until pink disappears) pour off drippings. Mix eggs and cheese together then add sausage. Spread mixture over dough. Top with remaining dough to form top crust. Place in oven approximately 20 minutes (till golden brown). Let cool slightly, cut into small, bitesize cocktail squares. Serve warm.

* * *

RAYMOND BERRY

Hall of Fame
New England Patriots
Receiver-Coach

HOT CHEESE BISCUITS

Great for luncheons.

1 lb. butter
1 lb. Old English sharp processed cheese
1½ loaves (approx.) sandwich bread—Pepperidge Farms

Beat butter and cheese 5 minutes. Take 3 slices bread, stack, decrust them. Cut into fourths. Ice each layer sides and top. Bake at 350⁰ 15—20 minutes until done. May be frozen before baking. Makes 40 biscuits.

Tampa Bay Buccaneers
Head Coach

JOHN H. McKAY

MEXICAN ROLLS

We serve these for hors d'oeuvres or with chili.

1 lb. grated sharp cheese (cheddar)
1 small garlic clove (minced)
2 cans chopped green chili peppers or
2 cans Ortega whole chili (seeds removed)—then chop (milder)
1 cup chopped black olives
2 T. vinegar
1 can enchilada sauce
18—24 french rolls or English muffins or small hard rolls

Combine all ingredients (except rolls). Split rolls—remove center and fill with mixture. Wrap rolls in foil. Heat oven 250° — 20—30 minutes if using English muffins—put mixture on muffin—then cut into fourths. Both may be frozen—to use when needed.

*   *   *

St. Louis Cardinals
12 Place Kicker

STEVE LITTLE

MICRO-WAVE NACHOS

2 Minutes in the micro wave and you have a quick appetizer that will keep them busy until the main course!

1 package Doritos
sliced cheddar cheese
hot taco sauce or tabasco
hot peppers

Place Doritos in pyrex dish, cover with sliced cheese, pour taco sauce over the cheese and drop on the peppers.

LAMAR McHAN

New Orleans Saints
Assistant Coach

PICKLED SHRIMP (New Orleans)

2—2½ lbs. raw shrimp
15—20 whole all spice
6—8 peppercorns
1/8 teas. black pepper
juice of ½ lemon
15—20 cloves
6 buds garlic, sliced
3 small onions, sliced

2 lg. bay leaves
2 pinches dried or 1 sprig fresh thyme
several sprigs of parsley
few bits dried red pepper
1 T. worcestershire sauce
4 med. onions, sliced thin
box of bay leaves
2 lg. stalks of celery,
crushed or broken

Season 2½ quarts of water with 3 T. of salt. Then add above ingredients except the shrimp, 4 onions and box of bay leaves. Bring to a boil and allow to simmer 20 minutes. Add shrimp and bring to boil again; simmer 12-15 minutes. Cool and devein shrimp. In a large pan, arrange the shrimp in layers with 4 medium sized onions sliced thin and the bay leaves. Pour over each layer the following sauce:

1¼ cups salad oil
¾ cup warmed white vinegar
1½ teas. salt
2½ teas. celery seed

2½ T. capers and juice
dash hot sauce
¼ cup worcestershire sauce
1 T. yellow mustard

After pouring sauce over shrimp, onions and bay leaves, cover pan and store in refrigerator 24 hours (or more). Serve with cocktail picks.

•   •   •

TOM TONER

Green Bay Packers
59 Linebacker

HOLIDAY NUTS

Great party snack.

Take desired amount of shelled pecans and saute in butter slowly until golden brown, over medium heat. Salt and allow to sit on brown paper bag to get rid of excess grease.

Chicago Bears Alumni
32 Quarterback

JOHN C. LUJACK

SPINACH BALLS

2 pkgs. frozen spinach, thawed and drained well
2 cups packaged stuffing mix
1 cup grated parmesan cheese
6 eggs, well beaten
¾ cup butter, softened
salt and pepper to taste

Combine all ingredients, mixing well. Roll into balls the size of walnuts. Freeze. Before serving, place on cookie sheet while still frozen. Bake 10 minutes at 350°. (60—70 balls)

• • •

Miami Dolphins
78 Defensive Lineman

CARL BARISICH

WALNUT CHEESE BALL

Delicious with crackers, rye bread, or bagel thins.

3 8 oz. pkgs. cream cheese
1 pkg. chipped (dried) beef, cut in small pieces
5 stalked scallions, chopped stalk and all
1 jigger milk
1 T. mayonnaise
chopped walnuts

Allow cream cheese to reach room temperature. Mix all ingredients well and form into ball. Roll in chopped nuts until completely covered. Chill.

TOMMY O'BOYLE

Kansas City Chiefs
Talent Scout

STUFFED OYSTERS

Since I am from New Orleans, I thought I would include a Recipe for stuffed oysters. This was made for my mama and our family by Nellie Law (who took care of me as a child) and who later cooked for me and my own family when Tommy was head coach at Tulane in New Orleans. If you have lots of time, this is the best appetizer for 6 people in the world. Rosemary.

2 dozen oysters and chop them up and save the juice (drain them in a colander) chop up 2 onions and 1 clove of garlic. Put into your iron skillet with 1 T. of lard and 1 bay leaf and a pinch of thyme, under low heat. Fry till the "onions clear" (are a pale yellow color). Add the chopped oysters. Stir gentle, easy-like. Take a cup of already toasted bread crumbs (from french bread) and wet with the oyster juice (liquid) you saved. Put that into the iron skillet, too. Fry for about 20 minutes till oysters "stop being watery". Add 2—3 T. butter and mix through with a fork, easy. (You have already boiled and scrubbed 6 oyster shells). Now you fill those with the mixture from your skillet. When you're almost ready to serve, sprinkle the tops of each shell with more bread crumbs, dot with butter and put in your oven till the butter melts and they're real hot. Serve right now!

*   *   *

DICK BIELSKI

Baltimore Colts
Tight-end Coach

PARTY SNACK

1 package Fritos
1 can jalapeno bean dip
1 can chilies peppers, hot
cheddar cheese

Crack Fritos into bite size pieces. Cover with bean dip and put small amount of cheese. Top with piece of hot pepper. Bake in slow oven 250° until cheese melts.

P.A.S.S. the Soup

WILLIAM SULLIVAN

CREAM ASPARAGUS SOUP

Broccoli can be substituted

With our hectic schedules, we enjoy cooking and eating this easy to prepare, foolproof, and delicious recipe. Mary.

1 to 2 lbs. asparagus
1 medium onion (chopped)
3 T. butter
3 cups of chicken broth
3 cups of light cream
3 T. of chopped chive

Saute chopped asparagus and onion in butter (about 5 minutes). Add chicken broth. Simmer for 20 minutes. Add cream. Put in blender and puree. Return to pan to keep warm. Float chopped chives on each cup or bowl of soup.

• • •

Washington Redskins
Special Teams Coach

JOHN HILTON

CHICKEN CORN SOUP

(Pennsylvania Dutch)

Cook whole chicken in large pot of water 2 or 3 hours to make good stock. Add chopped celery (3—4 stalks). Salt to taste. Hard boil 2—3 eggs, chop and add cut corn off cob (6—8 ears); add. Cook til corn is done.

PAUL RYCZEK

Atlanta Falcons
53 Center

PAUL'S HOMEMADE CHICKEN NOODLE SOUP

Passed down from Mom Helen. Good for what ails you. Great with saltines and sharp cheddar cheese and beer. Carol.

11 cups water	*egg drop noodles (dumplings):*
3—4 lb. cut up fryer	*3 eggs*
3—4 med. onion, sliced	*1½ cup flour*
3 carrots (opt.)	*1 teas. salt*
4 chicken boullion cubes	*milk (consistency should*
1—2 stalks celery & leaves	*be on sticky side, moist)*
1 T. freshly chopped parsley	
salt and pepper to taste	

Measure water, add salt, bring to boil. Drop in chicken, let boil again. Lower to medium heat. Add all ingredients except noodles. Allow to cook uncovered 45 minutes—1 hour. Seperate stock from chicken and vegetables (drain through colander). Set vegetable ingredients aside. Debone and skin chicken. Tear into spoonsize or bitesize pieces and set aside. Mix together noodle ingredients. Drop into broth (on low heat) by the teaspoonful. Cover and let cook for 10 minutes stirring occasionally. Add ingredients and set aside (chicken and vegetables). Turn off heat. Stir and serve.

• • •

MARVIN D. SWITZER

Buffalo Bills
21 Defensive Back—Safety

QUICK CHILI
(Quick Recipe)

Chop up 2 celery stalks, 1 medium onion, and 1 green pepper. Combine in skillet and cover with water. Cook until vegetables are soft. Cook over medium heat. In saucepan or crock pot, combine 2 cans of campbell's chili soup and 1½ cans of water. Heat over medium heat. Once vegetables become soft, add 1 lb of ground beef. Season with salt, pepper, garlic salt and chili powder. (Season to own liking.) Cook until ground beef is browned. Drain off grease. Add 2-8 oz. cans of tomato sauce and 1 pkg. of chili mix. Combine ground beef and vegetables to soup in sauce pan and cook low for one hour. You may add more chili powder as chili cooks.

CRAIG MORTON

CRAIG'S CHILI

This was quoted by Craig so seasoning measurements are sketchy. Very hot and serves multitudes! We always freeze some for later. Pass it!!! Susan.

2 lb. ground beef	*1½ T. oregano*
2 yellow onions	*1 jar hot chili peppers*
salt and pepper to taste	*1 reg. size bottle catsup*
3 T. chili powder	*2 or 3 cans kidney beans*
4 (1 lb.) cans whole, peeled tomatoes	

Brown ground beef and onions together with salt, pepper and 2 T. chili powder. Add 1 T. oregano. Add ½ jar of chili pepper juice. Simmer slightly. In separate big pot, mash 4 cans whole peeled tomatoes with hands. Add 2 or 3 cans kidney beans and 1 bottle catsup and remaining hot chili pepper juice. Add remaining oregano and chili powder and 1½ tomato cans of water. Pour beef mixture into pot and simmer 4 hours.

* * *

BOB KUECHENBERG

GRIDIRON CHILI

½ lb. dried pinto beans	*½ cup butter*
2 cans (16 oz.) tomatoes	*2½ lbs. ground chuck beef*
1 lb. green peppers coarsely chopped	*1 lb. pork (ground lean)*
1½ lb. onion coarsely chopped	*⅓ cup chili powder*
1½ T. salad oil	*2 T. salt*
2 cloves garlic, crushed	*1½ teas. pepper*
½ cup parsley, finely chopped	*1½ teas. ground cumin*

Wash beans, place in bowl and add water to two inches above beans. Soak overnight. Simmer, covered in the same water until tender. Add tomatoes and simmer for five minutes. Saute green peppers slowly in salad oil for five minutes. Add onion and cook until tender, stirring frequently. Add garlic and parsley. In large skillet melt butter and saute beef and pork for about 15 minutes. Add this mixture to beans and onions and season with salt, pepper, cumin, and chili powder. Then simmer, covered, for one hour. Remove cover and cook thirty minutes longer. Skim off fat at the top.

MAXIE BAUGHAN

Detroit Lions
Assistant Coach &
Defensive Co-ordinator

"LINEBACKER'S" CHILI

2 lbs. round steak
(cut in very small pieces)
3 lbs. ground round steak
4 med. onions-chopped
6 T. chili powder (may be adjusted to taste)
2 large cans tomatoes
1 small can tomatoes
2 T. red wine vinegar
1 10 oz. can chiles and tomatoes or
green chili salsa
(available in Old El Paso brand)
2 large cans kidney beans

5 T. bacon fat
5 cloves garlic
2 T. flour
5 bay leaves
2 T. salt
2 T. oregano
3 T. lt. brown sugar

Have a large heavy pot ready. Cut steak in very small pieces. Brown onions in bacon fat. Add pressed garlic. Brown all meat, drain and add to onions and garlic. Mix chili powder and flour, add to meat mixture and stir until smooth. Add tomatoes, which have been cut in small pieces and can of chiles and tomatoes. Cook gently for 20 minutes. Add bay leaves, salt, oregano, red vinegar and brown sugar. Cover and cook slowly for 2 hours. About 1 hour before serving, add two large cans red kidney beans.

•　　•　　•

JOE E. SPENCER

Kansas City Chiefs
Assistant Coach

TEXAS CHILI

3 lbs. ground beef
1 large onion
5 or 6 T. chili powder

2 cans tomatoes
2 cans chili beans,
if desired

Brown chopped onion in hot fat. Then brown ground beef. Add chili powder, tomatoes, and beans. Let simmer for an hour or two.

Buffalo Bills
52 Linebacker

DOUG BECKER

NANCY'S 2 QTS. CHILLI

1 lb. onions chopped
1/2 lb. ground beef suet
2 lbs. lean ground beef
1/2 teas. cinnamon
1/2 teas. cumin powder
1/2 teas. worcestershire sauce
3 toes garlic chopped
1 teas. chili powder
1 6 oz. tomato paste

1/2 teas. black pepper
1 teas. salt
1/2 teas. red pepper
1/2 teas. coriander powder
1 1/2 teas. vinegar
1/2 teas. ground allspice
3 bay leaves
1 qt. water
1 mexican pepper

Melt beef suet. Add chopped onions, cook slow heat for 3 hours. Then add meat and all ingredients, cook for 3 more hours. Serve with spaghetti, topped with chili, chili beans, shredded cheddar cheese and chopped fresh onions.

•   •   •

Pittsburgh Steelers
79 Offensive Tackle

LARRY BROWN

NEW ENGLAND CLAM CHOWDER

1/4 cup vegetable oil
2 medium onions, sliced
3 ten oz. cans of whole
   baby clams in broth
2 T. flour
1 T. butter

3 large potatoes, diced
2 teas. salt
1/4 teas. celery salt
1/2 teas. pepper
3 cups milk

Heat oil in dutch oven and cook onions several minutes over medium heat until tender. Chop clams. Save broth. Add enough water to broth to make 2 cups. Stir flour into onions and oil until blended. Add clam broth mixture slowly, stirring constantly until thickened. Stir in potatoes, salt, celery salt, and pepper. Cover and cook until potatoes are tender. Add clams, milk, and butter. Heat thoroughly, about 5 minutes, stirring constantly. Serves four to six, depending on size of servings.

MARK ARNESON

St. Louis Cardinals
57 Linebacker

SUPER EASY CLAM CHOWDER

1 large onion, chopped and sauteed in 1 stick margarine
(2 T. onion, 3 T. margarine)
6 cans Campbell's cream of potato soup (2 cans)
3 cans Doxsee clam chowder (1 can)
3-6½ oz. cans Doxsee minced clams (1 can);
drain and save liquid. Add to soup if it feels too thick.
2 qts. Half n' Half (1 pt. plus ½ cup)
salt and pepper to taste

Combine all ingredients and simmer in crock pot for 4 hours. Measurements in parentheses are amounts for 4 to 6 servings.

* * *

RUSTY JACKSON

Buffalo Bills
4 Punter

EGG DROP SOUP

Delicious.

4 cups chicken broth (made with bouillon cubes)
2 chopped green onions
2 raw eggs
1 small can chow mein noodles

Bring bouillon to boil. Add green onions to broth, let simmer until tender, then drop in 2 raw eggs breaking yellows. Let boil for 1 minute or until eggs are cooked. Serve broth mixture over chow mein noodles.

ANTHONY LEONARD

ANTHONY'S GUMBO

MEATS & SEA FOOD
2 Italian Sausages
(sliced ¼ in. thick)
2 smoked beef links
(sliced ¼ in. thick)
2 linguisia sausages
(sliced ¼ in. thick)
8 chicken wings
½ lb. small shrimp
(pre-cooked or frozen)
½ lb. lg. shrimp or prawns
(shelled & de-veined)
1 crab
½ lb. ham (cubed)
2 turkey wings

UTENSILS
x-large pot
skillet

VEGETABLES
1½ cups celery chopped
1½ cups green onions chopped
1 bell pepper chopped
½ yellow onion chopped
½ white onion chopped
3 cloves garlic chopped
1 green pepper sliced
1 lb. fresh okra or
2 packages frozen cut okra
rice, cooked

SEASONINGS
garlic powder
seasoning salt
pepper
2 beef bouillon cubes
2 chicken bouillon cubes
gumbo file

Boil chicken and turkey wings until the meat falls off the bones. After the meat is off the bones, remove as many bones from water as possible. While the chicken is boiling, brown sausages, links and linquisia, pour off excess grease. Pour sausages, ham into pot with chicken and turkey, let it boil for fifteen (15) minutes. Add all the vegetables to pot. Add seasoning to taste, and the bouillon cubes. Add more water if needed, must maintain a soup appearance. Let boil for one-half an hour. Now add your two (2) kinds of shrimp, boil for twenty (20) minutes. While the shrimp is doing its thing, you can make the "Rue". In the skillet melt two (2) tablespoons of grease until hot. Add to grease, 3 tablespoons flour, mix well, should look like a batter. If it doesn't, keep adding flour or grease until it does. Keep stirring, never stop, it will get hot. When it gets a dark golden brown color, remove from heat and add to pot. Quickly start stirring well, it should make it thicker, less soupy & browner in color. If it's still rather watery, mix a little flour and water together and add this to pot. Stir well. The Gumbo should be a little thinner than gravy. Add Crab later, let it boil for fifteen (15) minutes. Serve over cooked rice.

TERRY BRADSHAW

Pittsburgh Steelers
12 Quarterback

SEEFOOD GUMBO

This dish is also a favorite of Jerome Barkum, 83 Tight End, New York Jets.

1/2 cup shortening	1/2 cup flour
2 cups chopped okra	1 large onion
2/3 cup chopped celery	4 cloves garlic
1 cup crab meat	2 cups cleaned shrimp
2 teas. salt	2 qts. water
1 teas. worcestershire sauce	1/4 teas. red pepper sauce
2/3 cup green pepper	2 T. catsup

Melt shortening, add flour and brown. Add okra and saute until it ceases to rope. Add onion, celery, garlic and green pepper. Simmer about 10 minutes. Add shrimp, and crab meat and simmer until shrimp turn pink or about 15 minutes. Add hot water and seasonings. Bring to boil. Turn fire real low and let simmer about 1½ hours. Serve over rice.

• • •

TOM MYERS

New Orleans Saints
37 Free Safety

HEALTHY HAMBURGER SOUP

1 lb. ground chuck	1 cup red rose
1 teas. salt	1 cup water
2 med. potatoes, cut	2 cups tomato juice
2 med. onions, cut	1 (1 lb. 15 oz.) whole canned
1 cup carrots, sliced	tomatoes—cored, with juice
1 cup celery, sliced	1 8 oz. can stewed tomatoes
1 small can corn	2 bay leaves
1/2 green pepper, cut	salt, pepper to taste
1 small can mushrooms,	pinch oregano; pinch basil &
drained	any other spice you like

Cook meat in large stock pot until all pink is gone—sprinkle with salt. Pour off excess grease. Add rest of ingredients; cover and simmer at least 2 hours, or more. You may also add other vegetables you like—zucchini, beans, etc.

Baltimore Colts
10 Kicker

STEVE MIKE-MAYER

LECSO
(Hungarian)

Great when re-heated. Eat in a bowl or over rice and be sure to have a lot of fresh
french bread on hand to dip into it!

In a large pot: chop 6 medium onions and 4 bell peppers. Saute the chopped
onions in approximately 4 T. of oil. Add the green peppers. Add to that,
1—(2 lbs.) can of tomatoes, (but first chop the tomatoes). Add some hot
pepper seeds to spice it up and 2 T. of salt. Simmer for about ½ hour.

•   •   •

Kansas City Chiefs
3 Kicker

JAN STENERUD

BAKED FRENCH ONION SOUP

6 yellow onions thinly sliced
1 garlic clove, minced
1 stick butter
¼ teas. sugar
2 cans beef broth
1 soup can water
½ cup dry sherry
6 slices toasted french bread 1 inch thick
¾ cup gruyere cheese—freshly grated

In a saucepan saute the onions, sugar, garlic in the butter until lightly
browned. Add the broth, water and sherry. Simmer until the onions are
tender. Laddle soup into individual ovenproof crocks. Top each serving with
a slice of bread. Springle with cheese and bake at 375° until cheese has
melted.

CHESTER MARCOL

Green Bay Packers
13 Kicker

CROCK POT FRENCH ONION SOUP

3 cans consomme
2 cans water
2 T. flour
1 T. sugar
1 large sliced onion
½ packet dry onion soup
1 T. butter
croutons
swiss cheese

Brown onions in butter. Add flour and sugar. Add mixture to all liquid which is in crock pot. Stir in soup mix. Cook about 6 hours on low. To serve, ladle soup into soup crocks. Add croutons and place swiss cheese on top. Put in oven and bake until cheese melts.

•   •   •

**IN MEMORY OF
JOE CAMPANELLA**

Baltimore Colts
General Manager
73 Middle Guard

PASTAFASOLA
(Beans & Macaroni Soup)

Great for Fridays with pizza.

¼ cup oil   *1 can white kidney beans or navy*
½ onion, cut up   *salt and pepper to taste*
1 clove garlic   *pinch of parsley*
½ qt. tomatoes   *1 cup short macaroni*

Saute in oil, onion and garlic. Then add tomatoes and simmer ½ hour. Add 1 can beans and 1 can water. Let cook 1½ hours slowly. Boil 1 cup short macaroni and add to soup 10 minutes before serving. Garnish with Romano cheese. Serves 4.

Washington Redskins
54 Center

BOB KUZIEL

BEEF STEW

Cube Beef. Brown in oil. Add ½ cup cooking wine. Simmer until ½ way done. Precook potatoes and carrots. Drain, then add to stew beef. Add diced fresh peppers and celery. Finish cooking. 5 minutes before done, add 1 envelope of brown gravy mix (French's), dissolve with ½ cup of cold water. Mix well.

• • •

Cincinnati Bengals
34 Defensive Back

LOUIS BREEDEN

BRUNSWICK STEW
(Southern Style)

Good for when you have a lot of friends visiting and especially good for those cold winter nights. It's my grandmother's recipe which she always serves when the family gets together."

> *2 onions, chopped*
> *½ small cabbage, chopped*
> *2 cans (12) oz. tomatoes*
> *1 can (12) oz. drained lima beans*
> *1 can (12) oz. cream style corn*
> *1 qt. potatoes, diced*
> *hot sauce to taste (tabasco)*
> *salt to taste*
> *1 small hen*
> *2 lbs. of lean pork*

Cook hen and pork so tender that the meat falls off the bone. Cook potatoes tender enough to mash. Cook cabbage and onions the same way. Take broth from meat and add it to the mashed up potatoes, cabbage and onions. Put it all in large pot. Add other ingredients and cook until stew is thick over medium heat (1—1½ hours).

LYNN BRANDOM

Miami Dolphins

MAN PLEASING BEEF STEW

The savory cooking liquid is what makes the gravy and stew so distinctive. The addition of 7-up adds a flavor base that will surprise you.

2 teas. salt
¼ teas. pepper
1 teas. savory
1 teas. basil
1 teas. marjoram
½ cup flour
1½ lbs. beef chuck,
cut into 1½ in. cubes
6 T. bacon drippings

1 lg. onion, sliced
2 bottles (7 oz. ea.) 7-up
1 can whole tomatoes
1 beef bouillon cube
6 carrots, halved
6 med. potatoes, quartered
6 sm. zucchini, sliced
1 can (12 oz.) whole kernel corn

Combine salt, pepper, savory, marjoram, basil, and flour. Roll beef cubes in mixture. Brown beef slowly in bacon drippings. Add onion; cook until golden. Put meat and onion in large ovenproof casserole, leaving drippings in pan. Stir remaining seasoned flour into drippings. Slowly add 7-up, tomatoes, and bouillon cube, stirring well. Cook until thickened. Pour over meat; add carrots and potatoes. Cover and bake at 325° about 2½ hours. Add the zucchini and corn during last half hour of baking. Makes 6 to 8 servings.

• • •

ED BRADLEY

San Francisco Forty Niners
54 Linebacker

OYSTER STEW

1 qt oysters (3 doz.) strained
½ cup sliced mushrooms
2 cloves garlic, minced
3—4 stalks of celery, chopped
½ pt. heavy cream
½ teas. pepper

½ cup butter
1 med. onion, chopped
3 potatoes, cubed
1 teas. salt
2 pts. half & half cream

Saute oysters, onion, garlic and mushrooms in butter. Heat half & half and cream. Add oyster mixture, potatoes, celery, salt and pepper. Simmer until potatoes are tender. Serves 6—8.

Cincinnati Bengals
President
Hall of Fame

PAUL BROWN

OLD FASHIONED CHICKEN STEW

1 stewing chicken, 4—5 lbs.
4 zuccini, ¼ in. slices
1 pkg. carrots (about 12)
  cut in 4th's
2 turnips diced
1 bunch celery diced
(about 4 cups)

2 lg. onions chopped
(about 2 cups)
1 lg. can stewed tomatoes
2 teas. curry powder
3 cans cream of celery or
  cream of chicken soup

Put about 4 qts. of water in large cooker. Stew the chicken until tender. Remove from broth to bone and cool. Add the remaining ingredients to broth and cook until tender, about 45 minutes. Add the boned chicken and three cans of cream of celery or chicken soup. Bring to a boil and reduce the heat to off. Season with salt and pepper. Cook a 7 or 8 oz. package of noodles. Add to the stew.

*   *   *

Hall of Fame
Colts & Jets
Head Coach

WEEB EWBANK

WEEB'S FAVORITE OYSTER STEW
(From New Orleans)

1 pt. oysters w/liquid
1 lg. onion, sliced
¼ cup fresh parsley
¼ cup butter

1 T. worcestershire
salt, pepper & red pepper to taste
1½ qt. milk
½ cup cracker crumbs (opt.)

Saute onion in Butter. Add seasoning and strained liquid from oysters. Stir constantly to keep from curdling. Add oysters and simmer till edges curl. *Do Not Overcook!* Meantime, have milk heating slowly till scalded. Add above mixture to scalded milk and heat thoroughly. Serves 6.

JACK FERRANTE

Alumni
Philadelphia Eagles
83 End

VEAL SPEZZATE
(Stew)

2 lb. veal for stew (cubed)
1/2 cup oil
4 cloves garlic
1 cup peeled tomatoes
3 or 4 potatoes
1 pkg. frozen or 1 can sweet peas

salt
pepper
fresh parsley
rosemary leaves
celery

Salt and pepper meat. Brown cubes of meat in oil for 1/2 hour. Add garlic when garlic is golden remove from pan. Add tomatoes, rosemary leaves, celery and parsley. Cook until tomato is drawn. Peel and cube potatoes and boil in separate pot until tender. Drain. (Save some potatoe water.) Add to meat and tomato. Add some potatoe water to cover meat. Continue to simmer until drawn. About 3/4 hour. Salt to taste. Add cooked peas or canned peas. Bring to a boil. Serve with tossed salad. Pork may be used in place of veal.

• • •

FRANK GIFFORD

Hall of Fame
New York Giants
ABC Announcer
16 Running Back

VEGETABLE-CHEESE SOUP

2 cups chopped celery
1 cup chopped leeks
2 chopped scallions
2 cups chopped carrots
2 cups chopped (coarsely) broccoli

6 1/2 cups chicken broth
2 cups grated havarti cheese
3/4 cup heavy cream
dash cayenne

Boil vegetables in chicken broth just a few minutes. Mix together 2 T. of butter and 2 T. of flour into paste. Strain vegetables (but keep them!) Heat butter and flour mixture and pour broth into it gradually til slightly thick. Add vegetables, cheese, and cream. Heat til cheese is melted. Sprinkle cayenne.

P.A.S.S.
the
Salad

P.A.S.S.

Official

SBR

Sister Carol Ann

Chicago Bears &
Washington Redskins
75 Defensive Tackle

FRED WILLIAMS

BREAD & BUTTER PICKLES

12 medium cucumbers
6 small onions
½ cup rock salt
1½ qts. ice water
2 cups sugar
2 cups cider vinegar

1 teas. ginger
1 teas. cornstarch
2 teas. mustard seed
2 teas. mustard seed
½ teas. tumeric
½ teas. black pepper

Slice cucumbers and onions very thin (¼ inch orless). Soak for two hours in brine made up of salt and ice water to cover. Drain and rinse lightly. Meanwhile, combine remaining ingredients in kettle (not copper or iron) and boil one minute. When ready, add the soaked and drained cucumbers and onions and cook until beginning to boil. Pack into hot, sterile jars and seal.

• • •

Miami Dolphins
Offensive Coach

DAN HENNING

THREE BEAN SALAD

1 can cut green beans
1 can cut yellow wax beans
1 can red kidney beans
1 2 oz. jar pimentoes
¾ cup sugar

½ cup salad oil
1 cup vinegar
1 onion
1 green pepper

Rinse kidney beans in cold water. Drain well all beans and pimento. Cut pepper and onion in rings. (Separate pieces of onion.) Mix all together in large bowl. Chill.

HOWARD L. BRINKER

Cincinnati Bengals
Defensive Coordinator

BLUEBERRY MOLDED SALAD

1 pkg. blackberry jello
1 pkg. lemon jello
3½ cups boiling water
2 T. lemon juice (bottled or fresh)
1 can Thank You brand blueberries

Dilute jello in boiling water, add lemon juice and blueberries. Pour in individual molds and serve on lettuce. For dressing, use equal parts of cool whip and mayonnaise.

•   •   •

DON STROCK

Miami Dolphins
10 Quarterback

BROCCOLI AND CAULIFLOWER SALAD

1 bunch of broccoli
1 bunch of cauliflower
1 cup of cheddar cheese
juice from ½ fresh lemon
1 cup of swiss cheese
4 or 5 green onions
1 bottle of creamy cucumber dressing
salt and pepper

Chop broccoli and cauliflower. Chop green onions. Squeeze the lemon over the vegetables. Add the swiss and cheddar cheese. Salt and pepper to taste. Then pour salad dressing over salad and toss thoroughly. Refrigerate for several hours. Serves 6—8.

JACK DONALDSON

BROCCOLI 'N OLIVE SALAD

2 10 oz. pkgs. frozen chopped broccoli (thawed and drained)
1½ cups stuffed olives, sliced finely
1 medium onion chopped
6 hard cooked eggs, chopped
1 can (5 oz.) water chestnuts, drained and sliced
½ cup mayonnaise or enough
½ cup bean sprouts (opt.)

Combine broccoli, olives, onion, eggs and water chestnuts. Coat with mayonnaise. Serve chilled in bowl or melon shell.

•   •   •

Green Bay Packers
88 Tight End
Alumni

RON KRAMER

CAESAR SALAD

2 heads of romaine lettuce
¼ cup wine vinegar
¼ cup Italian olive oil
½ teas. dry mustard
1 teas. worcestershire sauce

½ teas. garlic
1 can anchovey
½ lemon squeezed
¼ teas. ground pepper
3 T. parmesan cheese

Clean two heads of romaine lettuce, wrap in towel and refrigerate for 2 hours. Put all ingredients except lettuce, in blender and mix. When ingredients are blended sufficiently, pour into a very large bowl. Coddle two eggs and then add to ingredients and mix. Break lettuce with hand (do not cut!) and mix with the ingredients. Add croutons, cracked pepper and parmesan cheese to your liking.

BRAD DUSEK

Washington Redskins
59 Linebacker

SWEET AND SOUR GREEN SALAD

This makes a lot of dressing and may be halved. May be used for other type salads as well.

spinach leaves and/or romaine lettuce *   bean sprouts (opt.)
mushrooms, sliced   hard-boiled egg(s), chopped
manderin oranges   spring onions, chopped
almond slivers   bacon bits, just a few croutons

Clean and dry greens. Combine all ingredients and toss gently.

DRESSING

1 cup oil   ¾ cup red wine vinegar
1 cup sugar   dash of salt
½ cup catsup

Combine all ingredients and mix well, preferably in a blender. Chill. *More attractive if both are used.

●   ●   ●

TED PLUMB

Chicago Bears
Receiver Coach

CANTALOUPE SALAD

Ted's favorite summer salad.

1 cantaloupe diced
1 carton cottage cheese (drained)
1 pkg. orange jello
1 small carton cool whip

Mix diced cantaloupe and cottage cheese. Sprinkle dry jello over mixture and stir well. Add cool whip and chill.

Hall of Fame
New York Giants
4 Fullback

**IN MEMORY OF
"TUFFY" LEEMANS**

CRANBERRY SALAD MOLD

1 3 oz. raspberry gelatin
1 cup of boiling water
1 16 oz. can whole cranberries
1 8 oz. can crushed pineapple (including juices)
½ cup cold water (dissolve 1 envelope plain gelatin)
chopped nuts can be added if desired

Dissolve gelatin in boiling water. Combine with other ingredients. Stir well. Turn into mold. Use with sour cream as a topping. (You can double recipe if desired.)

•　•　•

Seattle Seahawks
81 Tight-End

JOHN SAWYER

PINK FRUIT SALAD

1 can cherry pie filling
1 can chunk pineapple
1 can mandarin oranges
1 can Eagle Brand sweet condensed milk
1 9 oz. cool whip

Drain fruit, add pie filling, sweet condensed milk and cool whip. Mix very well and chill overnight or at least 6—8 hours. (Tastes better when chilled overnight.) Serve.

JOHNNY SQUARE

Minnesota Vikings
89 Wide Receiver,
Punt & Kick-off Returner

MEXICAN SALAD

1 head lettuce, torn into bite size pieces
1 lb. lean ground beef, fried loose and drained
2 large tomatoes, cut into bite size pieces
½ cup chopped celery
½ cup chopped onion
1 can red kidney beans, drained or 1—2 cups cooked pinto beans
1 8 oz. pkg. tortilla chips, crushed
2 cups shredded cheese, cheddar
1 avocado, slivered
1 cup sunflower seeds
1 large bottle Thousand Island dressing

Toss all ingredients together in a large bowl, using desired amount of Thousand Island dressing.

* * *

ROD PERRY

Los Angeles Rams
49 Defensive Back

QUICK JELLO/COTTAGE CHEESE SALAD

1 3 oz. pkg. jello (any flavor)
1 cup cottage cheese
1 cup cool whip
1 small can crushed pineapple drained
1 can mandarin oranges, drained and cut in small pieces

In a bowl, put cottage cheese and cool whip, sprinkle dry jello over this and mix well, and add drained fruits to mixture. Keep chilled until serving time. Ready to eat almost instantly.

HERMAN SARKOWSKY

MUSHROOM-ZUCCHINI SALAD

½ lb. fresh mushrooms sliced
1 avacado, peeled & diced
1 zucchini, thinly sliced
1 tomato diced
¼ cup sliced scallions
1 teas. sugar
1 teas. salt
½ teas. coarsly ground black pepper
½ teas. marjoram leaves, crumbled
4 T. salad oil
2 T. white vinegar
lettuce leaves

In a salad bowl, combine mushrooms, avacado, zucchini, tomato and scallions. Sprinkle with sugar, salt, black pepper and marjoram. Toss gently. Add oil and vinegar; toss until well coated. Serve on lettuce-lined salad plates. Serves 6.

* * *

Cincinnati Bengals
11 Quarterback

JOHN REAVES

MANDARIN COCONUT BOWL

Combine one 1 pound 4½ ounce can pineapple tidbits, drained, one 11 ounce can mandarin oranges, drained, 1 cup seedless green grapes, 1 cup miniature marshmallows, and 1 cup flaked coconut. Fold in 1 cup dairy sour cream. Chill overnight. Serve in lettuce cups. Makes 8 servings.

DAN ROONEY

Pittsburgh Steelers
President

ORANGE & SPINACH SALAD

2 lbs. fresh spinach—washed, dried, & stems removed
  tear into bite-sized pieces
1 lb. fresh mushrooms—washed, dried, and sliced thinly
4 eating (not juice) oranges—peel, separate sections,
  slice each section into 4 pieces
1 large Bermuda (red) onion—slice thinly, separate rings

DRESSING

1 cup olive oil	2 heaping T. mayonnaise
1/3 cup wine vinegar	1 teas. McCormick's Season-All
1 T. sugar	1/2 teas. tarragon
1/2 teas. oregano	1 clove garlic minced or
1/2 teas. salt	1 teas. garlic powder
1/2 teas. pepper	2 T. lemon juice

Toss all salad ingredients with dressing. These amounts make a very large salad—serves approximately 10 or 12.

• • •

BILL ARNSPARGER

Miami Dolphins
Defensive Coach

RICE SALAD

2 cups cooked rice	1/4 cup red wine vinegar
1 bell pepper, chopped	1/2 cup oil
3 tomatoes	1 1/2 teas. salt
2 T. minced onion	1/2 teas. garlic powder
2 T. parsley flakes	pepper to taste

Use long grain converted rice, cook according to directions. Vegetables may be chopped in blender, food processor or by hand. Mix altogether in large bowl with rice, vinegar, oil and seasonings. Chill and serve. Serves 6.

SID LUCKMAN

PEPPERONI SALAD

This is a spicy main course salad.

3 pkgs. 8 oz. Kraft Mozzarella cheese
5 mild pepperoni—unsliced
1 large red onion
2 bunches scallions
2 cans black olives (pitted)
3 pkgs. frozen salad shrimp
1 large pkg. Kraft shredded cheddar cheese
¼—1¼ cup mayonnaise
1 small bottle chili sauce
dash garlic salt

Julienne cheese, slice pepperoni (¼ inch slices), slice onions very thin, chop scallions. Toss mayonnaise, chili sauce and garlic salt with the remaining ingredients. All ingredients can be prepared early in the day—refrigerate separately and combine when ready to serve. Add sauce at serving time.

•   •   •

Atlanta Falcons
14 Quarterback

JUNE JONES, III

SPINACH SALAD

2 lbs. raw spinach greens (tear in bite size pieces)
¼ lb. crisped and chopped (can use a little more) bacon
4 hard boiled eggs—chopped or shredded

DRESSING

⅓ cup olive oil
⅓ cup Wesson oil
1 T. salt
⅓ cup wine vinegar

½ teas. pepper, ground
1 clove garlic, crushed
1 teas. monosodium glutamate

Shake several times before using. Toss and serve.

HOWARD SCHNELLENBERGER

Miami Dolphins
Alumni

PAR-EXCELLENCE STRAWBERRY JELLO

This jello mold is wonderful to eat with the meal or as a dessert. We love to add it to a backyard barbecue as a delicious change. Once our family has a taste of this jello delight, it disappears very quickly!

3 cups boiling water
1 cup cool water
3 small pkgs. strawberry jello
2 10 oz. pkgs. frozen strawberries
1 ✓2 can crushed pineapple
1 pt. sour cream
1 or 2 bananas

Dissolve jello in boiling water. Add cool water. Let cool. Add berries, juice, and crushed pineapple. Let ½ mixture congeal (slightly in 9x12 baking dish). Spread sour cream over this layer then slice bananas and place on top of sour cream. Top with rest of jello. Refrigerate until firm.

•   •   •

JIMMY ROBINSON

San Francisco 49er's
85 Wide Receiver

WATERGATE SALAD

Quick and easy. Good with a shrimp dish.

1 pkg. pistachio instant pudding
8 or 9 oz. cool whip
1 20 oz. can crushed pineapple
½ cup mini-marshmallows
½ cup chopped walnuts

To pudding, stir in cool whip. Add remaining ingredients. Stir all ingredients. Place in a long dish and refrigerate for 15 minutes.

Baltimore Colts   **FRED SCHUBACH**
Player Personnel Director

TWENTY-FOUR HOUR SALAD

This salad will stay fresh and crisp for quite a few days.

In a 9x13 pan, layer the following in exact order:

1 medium head lettuce, broken up
3 stalks celery, diced
1 medium onion, sliced
1 can water chestnuts, diced
1 small pkg. frozen peas
cover with mayonnaise
sprinkle 3 T. sugar
cover with parmesan cheese
3 or 4 hard boiled eggs, diced
2 or 3 tomatoes, diced
½ lb. bacon, crisply cooked and crumbled on top

Cover lightly and refrigerate for 24 hours before serving. When serving do not spoon up—cut with a spatula and cut through from top to bottom so each guest will benefit from all of the ingredients.

•   •   •

Denver Broncos   **RON EGLOFF**
Tight End

FRENCH DRESSING

1½ cup oil, beat 10 minutes alone and add:
1 cup sugar
1 T. prepared mustard
1 T. salt
1 teas. pepper
1 teas. paprika, beat 2 more minutes and add:
1 T. grated onion
¾ cup white vinegar
1 can tomato soup

Beat all for 1 minute more. Makes 1 quart.

JIM OTIS

St. Louis Cardinals
35 Running Back

JIM'S FAVORITE SALAD DRESSING

This recipe is a great testimony of why my waistline expands in the off season.

1/3 cup white vinegar
1/2 cup sugar
1 teas. salt
1 teas. worcestershire
1/2 medium onion, chopped
1 cup vegetable oil

Mix all your ingredients in a blender or food processor until creamy. Great on any type of salad.

* * *

ROB HERTEL

Cincinnati Bengals
16 Quarterback

A THOUSAND ISLAND DRESSING

Will keep many days in refrigerator.

1 1/2 cups mayonnaise
1/2 cup catsup
1/2 cup pickle relish
1 small can black olives, chopped
2 hard boiled eggs, diced

In large bowl, stir mayonnaise to make it smooth. Add the catsup and stir. Add small can chopped olives, hard boiled eggs and relish. Makes 1 qt.

Minnesota Vikings
22 Free Safety

PAUL KRAUSE

ROQUEFORT DRESSING

1 pint mayonnaise
½ pint sour cream
1 pinch garlic powder
1 T. lemon juice
1 pkg. blue cheese

Blend in mixer. Store in refrigerator.

•   •   •

Kansas City Chiefs
Assistant Coach

O. KAY DALTON

TOMATO RELISH

This relish recipe was handed down in my husband's family for years and found its way to our home. We love it to complement meats and chicken or mix it with a B-B-Q for a sweet, delicious sauce. I use my husband's home grown tomatoes, onions and peppers and seal with love. Mary Jane.

30 med. tomatoes
12 tart apples
1 pt. vinegar
3 sweet green peppers
1 teas. allspice
½ teas. cloves

10 med. onions
3 cups sugar
5 T. salt
3 sweet red peppers
1 teas. cinnamon

Core apples but do not peel. Put apples, peppers, and onions thru food grinder. Scald and peel tomatoes. Cut fine and mix with apple mixture. Add remaining ingredients and cook until thick, or 1 hour after it boils. Put into hot sterilized jars. (Stir often as this will scorch.) Makes 8—10 pints.

ALEX WOJCIECHOWICZ

Hall of Fame
Detroit & Philadelphia
53 Center and Linebacker

POLISH PICKLES

2 medium sized cucumbers
2 scallions (use green tops also)
sprig of fresh dill
salt
4 T. sugar (to taste)
½ cup white vinegar

Peel cucumbers and slice thinly. Chop scallions and green tops, then add to cucumbers. Add dill which has been chopped up. Sprinkle with a small amount of salt, cover with water, and put in refrigerator for an hour or two. Pour off water. Add vinegar and sugar and keep mixing until taste is not too tart or too sweet. Chill and serve.

MIKE KIRKLAND

DAD'S OZARK BAR-B-Q SAUCE

Ozark country is famous for its great smoked meats, and this original sauce created by my father-in-law is **super** on any smoked meats, and **great** in baked beans.

1 large onion, chopped
1½ sticks melted margarine
1 cup packed dark brown sugar
14 oz. prepared mustard
3 oz. liquid smoke
1 or 2 teas. garlic powder
32 oz. catsup
1 can Rotel
6 oz. worcestershire sauce
½ cup lemon juice
1 teas. celery seed
1½ teas. oregano
1 cup water

Saute onion in margarine until tender—add brown sugar, mix well. Add remaining ingredients, bring to a boil, and simmer one hour. Strain, pour into jars and refrigerate.

*   *   *

RON JESSIE

RON & SHARI'S ALOHA SAUCE

We like to use this sauce to marinate chicken overnight. We then either bake it in the sauce, or bar-b-que and baste with remaining sauce. It's equally good for fish or to make teriyaki beef. Good for 1½ to 2 lbs. meat. ALOHA!

½ cup salad oil
½ cup soy sauce
¼ cup honey
2 T. fresh ginger

2 teas. ground ginger
2 cloves minced garlic
2 T. chopped green onions

Mix together.

RAY HAMILTON

New England Patriots
71 Nose Tackle

DOWN-HOME RIBS

4 lbs. spareribs
¾ cup catsup
2 T. worcestershire sauce
2 T. vinegar
1½ cups water
2 T. brown sugar
1½ teas. salt
1 teas. chili powder
¼ teas. pepper
1 medium onion, chopped
1 clove garlic, crushed

Cut ribs between bones to make individual ribs. Place in single layer in large shallow pan and bake in preheated 350° oven for ½ hour. Meanwhile, combine remaining ingredients and bring to a boil; simmer 5 minutes and remove from heat. Drain fat from ribs. Pour warm sauce over ribs and bake about 1 hour turning and basting occasionally with sauce in pan. Serves 4.

● ● ●

JOE COLLIER

Denver Broncos
Defensive Co-ordinator

OUTDOOR BARBEQUE SAUCE FOR CHICKEN OR RIBS

Great when cooked on charcoal grill.

1 cup Open Pit barbeque sauce
⅓ cup maple syrup
3 T. soy sauce
dash worcestershire sauce
dash tabasco
1 teas. Kitchen Bouquet

52—Souper Bowl of Recipes

JOE DE LAMIELLEURE

BARBECUE SAUCE FOR SPARERIBS OR SHORT RIBS

2 T. vinegar
2 T. sugar
3 T. worcestershire sauce
1 cup ketchup
2 T. oil

Heat together above ingredients until blended. Pour over browned ribs. Bake ¾ hour at 350° covered.

*   *   *

CHARLIE CONERLY

CHARLIE CONERLY'S SPAGHETTI WITH CLAM SAUCE

Charlie frequently makes his own pasta.

½ cup chopped parsley
1 lb. spaghetti
3 T. olive oil
3 T. butter
juice from 1 can clams

1 clove garlic, minced
2 cans (7½ oz. cans) minced clams
juice of 1 lemon
½ cup dry white wine

Start spaghetti first. Drop into big (at least 4 qt.) pot of boiling, salted water to which 1 T. of olive oil has been added. Boil about 10 minutes. While spaghetti boils, prepare the sauce: put 3 T. olive oil in large skillet, heat, add garlic and stir. Add juice from one can of clams and the parsley. Add the two cans of drained clams. Stir till hot but not boiling, as boiling toughens the clams. Add the lemon juice, wine, salt and pepper to taste. Drain spaghetti and toss with 3 T. butter in warm serving dish. Pour sauce over and top with parmesan cheese. Preparation time: 15 minutes.

PAT PEPPLER

Houston Oilers
Assistant General Manager

SPECIAL MARINADE FOR LONDON BROIL

1½ cup salad oil
4 T. worcestershire sauce
2 T. dry mustard
2 teas. salt
2 teas. coarse black pepper

¾ cup soy sauce
½ cup wine vinegar
2 teas. dry parsley flakes
2 cloves garlic, crushed
⅓ cup lemon juice

Marinate meat (preferably flank steak) overnight. Broil (preferably char-broil) to suit (rare, etc.) [It is better to undercook, because meat cooks while being kept warm.] Slice at an angle and collect the essence. Add the essence to the marinade and put the slices in this sauce in a warm oven temporarily. If delayed in serving slices cool rapidly. This will also cook the meat if it is not well enough done. Another recipe (marinade) that is simpler and not quite as sharp is ½ Italian to ½ French salad dressing. Marinate and prepare as above.

*   *   *

TIM FOLEY

Miami Dolphins
25 Safety

VEGETABLES & CHEESE SAUCE

Eating is a favorite pastime of mine—I pray mightily for a higher metabolism!!!

Boil an assortment of fresh vegetables. Serve with cheese sauce made from medium white sauce recipe with 1½ cups grated cheese.

Green Bay Packers
50 Middle Linebacker

JIM CARTER

PRE-PARTY HOLLANDAISE SAUCE

This cannot curdle and can be stored days ahead.

3 egg yolks
½ teas. salt
1/8 teas. cayenne pepper

¼ lb. butter
1½ T. lemon juice
2 T. boiling water

Beat egg yolks until light. Add salt and pepper. Melt butter and separately heat lemon juice. Alternately add a little of each to egg yolk, beating constantly and *fast*. Continue beating, slowly adding boiling water. (I simply use a blender.) If desired, store in refrigerator. Before serving, soften in a double boiler over warm water.

*   *   *

Washington Redskins
26 Defensive Halfback

ANDY DAVIS

HOT FUDGE SAUCE

1 cup sugar
3 heaping T. Hershey's cocoa
1 T. butter
1 can evaporated milk
1 teas. vanilla

Blend sugar and cocoa together and heat slowly on top of stove. When sugar and cocoa are very hot, add butter and blend. Then add milk and stir well. Add 1 teas. vanilla. Boil about 4—5 minutes. Serve over favorite ice-cream.

CLYDE "BULLDOG" TURNER

Hall of Fame
Chicago Bears
66 Center-Linebacker

HOT MUSTARD

1 cup dry mustard (Coleman Hot)   1 cup sugar
1 cup vinegar   2 eggs
1 teas. salt

Put mustard in vinegar overnight. Add eggs, sugar, salt, and cook to a custard thickness. Serve with turkey, ham, etc.

* * *

MATTHEW ROBINSON

New York Jets
17 Quarterback

STRAWBERRY SAUCE FOR PANCAKES

1 pkg. (1 lb. frozen whole strawberries
1/2 cup currant jelly

Combine strawberries (thaw them—do not drain) and jelly. Stir over low heat for 10 minutes.

* * *

DON SHULA

Miami Dolphins
Head Coach

WINE SAUCE FOR STEAKS

1 cup mushrooms, canned or fresh   4 teas. cornstarch
1/4 cup chopped onion   3/4 cup burgundy cooking wine
1/4 cup butter   3/4 teas. salt
2 T. snipped parsley   dash of pepper

Cook over medium heat in a medium to medium large skillet. Melt butter first, then add onions, mushrooms, salt, pepper, parsley, cornstarch and wine, in that order. Delicious with any beef or even veal.

P.A.S.S.
the
Main Course

TOM KEANE

Miami Dolphins
Def. Backfield Coach

ELEPHANT STEW

1 medium size elephant
2 rabbits (optional)
salt and pepper

Cut elephant in bite size pieces. Add enough brown gravy to cover. Cook over kerosene fire about 4 weeks at 450°. Serves 3,800 people. If more people are expected, add 2 rabbits. Do this only in emergency as most people don't like hare in their stew.

Hall of Fame
Pittsburgh Steelers
Detroit Lions
Washington Redskins
35 Half Back

BILL DUDLEY

BEEF BAR-B-Q FOR BUNS

Spooned from wide mouthed thermos, on finger rolls, great for tail-gating.

1—6 lb. chuck roast (or round tip)	*3 T. bar-b-q sauce*
1 stalk celery, chopped	*1 T. vinegar*
3 large onions, chopped	*1 T. salt*
1 green pepper, chopped	*1 t. pepper*
1 bottle catsup	*1½ cup water*

Cut beef into 5 or 6 pieces. Combine other ingredients and heat to boiling point. Cover and bake in heavy pan, at 300°, for 6 hours or til tender enough to flake. If sauce is too thin, cook down. Prepare a day or two before using. Store in refrigerator and reheat as needed. (Also freezes well if made in larger quantities.)

* * *

Minnesota Vikings
President

MAX WINTER

BRISKET OF BEEF

Place brisket in heavy duty foil. Pour a mixture of brown sugar, package of Liptons onion soup and enough orange juice to moisten the misture and pat it on top of the meat and seal tightly. Bake at 325° for 2½ hours. Cool and slice. Put slices in pyrex dish with juices and bake ½ hour, uncovered.

TONY CANADEO

Hall of Fame
Green Bay Packers
3 Halfback

BEEF BURGUNDY

2 lbs. beef chuck, cut in 1 in. cubes
1—2 cups sliced onions (I use 2 cups)
3 T. flour
1/8 teas. marjoram
1/8 teas. thyme
1¼ teas. salt
¼ teas. pepper
1 can consomme
1 cup burgundy wine
½ lb. fresh mushrooms cut in half

Brown meat on all sides in butter. Sprinkle flour and seasoning over meat and stir in consomme and wine. Cover and simmer for 1½ hours. Saute onions in butter, add to meat and simmer ¾ hour. Saute mushrooms. Add to kettle and simmer an additional 15 minutes. Serve over noodles, rice or potatoes.

•   •   •

JEFF SIEMON

Minnesota Vikings
50 Middle Linebacker

TAGLIARINI

(Casserole)

1 med. onion   *1 pkg. noodles*
1 lb. ground beef   *2 cups grated cheddar or Colby cheese*
1 lg. can creamed corn (10 oz.)   *1 T. chili powder*
1 can tomatoes (any kind) don't drain   *garlic salt to taste*
1 can pitted olives (cut up) drained   *pepper to taste*

Brown ground beef and chopped onion til just cooked. Salt and pepper. Add chili powder, corn, tomatoes and olives. Cook over med. heat 20 minutes. Cook noodles as directed. Drain water and put in casserole. Add cheese and stir around til mixed. Add combined ingredients and put in 350° oven uncovered for 30—45 minutes.

58—Souper Bowl of Recipes

New England Patriots
General Manager

FRANK KILROY
"BUCKO"

CALVIN KLEIN BEEF BOURGUIGNON

2 lbs. cubed steak
1/2 teas. pepper
1 bunch parsley
3 T. olive oil
2 T. brandy
1—2 white onions
2 cups beef broth

1/2 teas. salt
dash of thyme
1/2 bay leaf
2 cups red burgundy
butter
1/4 lb. sliced mushrooms
2 cloves, garlic, mashed

In a bowl, place meat, add salt, thyme, pepper, parsley, bay leaf, olive oil, wine and brandy. Marinate the meat in this mixture 4 hours in the refrigerator. Strain and dry meat, reserving the marinade. Saute onions in butter in a heavy skillet until golden. Remove. Fry mushrooms until golden, then return onions to pan. In another pan, saute meat until very brown, continuously removing the grease. Bring beef broth to a boil and add to the meat. Pass marinade through a sieve and add to meat with the garlic. Cook until meat is tender. Add mushrooms and onions to meat and cook, covered, another 30 minutes. Serves 6 to 8.

* * *

Seattle Seahawks
Owner

ELMER NORDSTROM

CORNED BEEF CASSEROLE

This recipe is very easy. Serves 12 — 14.

3 cans Libby corned beef
3 cans Campbells mushroom soup
1 12 oz. pkg. of med. noodles

1 med. green pepper, ground
1 med. sized onion
12 pieces bacon, crumbled

Cook noodles. Put corned beef in large skillet. Add soup, mix together. Stir in green pepper and onion (ground together) and bacon. I use a roasting pan to mix above ingredients with noodles. Place in 4 qt. casserole. Top with a 2 inch thick layer of grated cheddar cheese. Bake at 325° until heated through, about 45—60 minutes, test center to be sure it is hot.

JIMMY WEBB

San Francisco 49ers
74 Defensive Tackle

EL DORADO BEEF-CHEESE CASSEROLE

1 lb. lean ground beef
1 T. instant minced onions
½ T. garlic salt
1 small can chopped green chillies drained
1 pkg. 7 oz. tortilla chips
2 cups (½ lb.) grated Monterey Jack cheese

2—8 oz. cans tomato sauce
1 cup sour cream
1 cup cottage cheese

Brown beef. Drain fat. Add onion, garlic salt and tomato sauce. Combine sour cream, cottage cheese and green chillies. Crush tortilla chips slightly. Place ½ chips in greased 2½ qt. casserole. Add ½ meat mixture, then ½ cream mixture, then cheese. Repeat. Bake uncovered at 350° for 30—35 minutes. Serves 6.

* * *

GARY HUFF

Tampa Bay Buccaneers
19 Quarterback

BEEF AND GREEN CHILES CASSEROLE

Grand Prize winner for Tampa Times Recipe Contest Cookoff.

1 to 1½ lbs. ground beef (chuck or round preferred)
1 dozen flour tortillas
1 can cream of mushroom soup
1 can cream of chicken soup
1 small container (8 oz.) sour cream
1 small can chopped green chilies
1 med. onion, chopped
cheddar cheese, grated

Brown ground beef. Drain off fat. Mix and heat cream of mushroom soup, cream of chicken soup, sour cream and chilies. (Don't use whole chilies that you chop yourself—they're too hot.) Layer in 2½ qt. casserole dish: tortillas (4 to 6 for each layer), ground beef, soup and chilies mixture, onion. Repeat layers and top casserole with cheese. Bake at 350° for 20 minutes.

60—Souper Bowl of Recipes

Denver Broncos   **GERRY H. PHIPPS**
Chairman, Board of Directors

BEEF CHASSEUR A LA MODE

*2 10 oz. sirloin steaks—charcoal broiled—very rare
   cut into ½—¾ inch cubes
noodles—about same amount—cooked until not quite done
1 can Campbell's cream of mushroom soup
¼ lb. butter
½ cup half and half cream
½ cup sour cream
worcestershire sauce
port wine*

In large saucepan over light fire, melt butter, add soup, stir until mixed and simmering. Add meat, stir until simmering. Then add noodles and stir until simmering, add half and half, stir and simmer. Add sour cream, stir and simmer, add dash of worcestershire, stir. Add about 2 T. port wine, stir and serve. Serves 4.

•   •   •

Atlanta Falcons   **BRENT ADAMS**
61 Offensive Tackle

CHINESE PEPPER STEAK

*1½ lb. steak, cut into thin strips   1 T. sherry
   (round if tender, sirloin best)   1/8 teas. garlic powder
2 T. oil   2 T. cornstarch
salt to taste   ¼ teas. ground ginger
1 green pepper, cut into strips   3 T. water
1 onion chopped   1 tomato cut into wedges (opt.)
1 T. soy sauce   hot cooked rice*

Quickly brown meat in hot oil. Add salt, green pepper, onion, soy sauce, sherry, garlic powder, and ginger. Cover, cook on low for 10 minutes. Combine cornstarch and water. Add to thicken. Add tomatoes, if desired. Serve over hot cooked rice.

CHRIS HANBURGER

Washington Redskins
55 Right Linebacker

CHOP SOUPY

This recipe freezes well. It is excellent for after a game as it can be made ahead and reheated. Served with a salad and hot bread, it is a complete meal.

1 lb. round stead	2 T. salad oil
cut in thin strips	sliced fresh tomatoes
1½ cups diagonally sliced celery	½ cup green onion
½ cup green pepper,	sliced, stems chopped
cut in 1 inch strips	2 T. soy sauce
1 can beef broth	½ cup water
2 T. cornstarch	1 cup bean sprouts
1 small can water chestnuts, sliced	drained and rinsed
4 oz. can sliced mushrooms	

Brown steak in oil in large skillet; add vegetables, broth and soy sauce. Mix cornstarch and water, add to other ingredients and stir well. Cover; cook over low heat for 20 minutes or until meat is tender. Serve over onion rice.

• • •

GARY FAMIGLIETTI

Alumni
Boston Yanks 1946
Player Coach

FAMIGLIETTI'S BRACIOLE

3 lb. thin sliced top of the round steak	1 teas. salt
1 cup fresh chopped parsley	½ teas. pepper
1 cup hand grated romano cheese	1 teas. onion salt
1 teas. garlic salt	

Flatten steak and trim off all fat. Cut into strips about 3 inches wide. Sprinkle meat with chopped parsley, cheese and seasonings. Roll and tie securely with string. Brown in hot olive oil. Add braciole (meat rings) to spaghetti sauce and cook till tender. Serve with spaghetti.

Green Bay Packers
84 Wide Receiver &
Kick Return Specialist

STEVE ODOM

ENCHILADAS

Spicy and great! Serve with tossed green salad and lots of iced fruit punch.

1—1½ lb. ground beef
1 onion chopped
large can refried beans
½—1 jar hot taco sauce

Brown hamburger and onion. Add beans and taco sauce to taste. Soften flour tortillas in hot oil. Blot between paper towels. Pour 1—15 oz. can mild enchilada sauce in bottom of 9x13 pan. Fill tortillas with a scoop of meat mixture, roll, and place in pan. Top with one more can mild enchilada sauce. Cover with cheddar cheese, grated. Bake 15 minutes at 350⁰. Serve with sour cream. Makes 17 small or 12—15 large enchiladas, depending on size of tortillas.

•   •   •

Seattle Seahawks
18 Punter

HERMAN WEAVER

FLANK STEAK WITH PARMESAN SAUCE

Tenderize flank steak. (May also be marinated in Good Seasons garlic dressing made to packets instructions.) Cook on grill to desired doneness. Cut on bias in strips about 1 inch wide. Spoon sauce over each strip and serve on platter.

SAUCE

1 stick butter—may want more, depending on desired
thickness
¾ cup parmesan cheese
¼ cup minced green onion

Melt butter in sauce pan, add parmesan cheese and minced green onion. Cook over low heat, stirring frequently for about 10 minutes.

STEVE WILSON

Tampa Bay Buccaneers
50 Center

SPIKED HAMBURGERS

These are by far the best hamburgers I've ever eaten and nothing tops off a good meal like a delicious dessert.

1 lb. ground beef	*1 T. dry onion flakes*
½ cup bread crumbs	*1 teas. prepared horseradish*
¼ cup dry red wine	*1 teas. dijon style mustard*
3 T. chili sauce	*1 teas. worcestershire sauce*
½ teas. salt	*1/8 teas. garlic powder*
1/8 teas. pepper	

Combine all ingredients. Grill about 6 minutes for medium. Makes 6 to 8 patties.

• • •

BILL McPEAK

New England Patriots
Personnel

GERMAN POT ROAST
(Use Dutch Oven)

4 lbs. bottom round	*1 teas. pepper*
¼ cup crisco	*1½ cups hot water*
1 chopped onion	*flavor to taste*
2 teas. salt	

Heat oil in dutch oven (medium heat). Season meat, then brown on each side. Remove from pan and brown onion. Remove oil from pan. Add hot water, bring to boil, then lower flame to simmer. Return meat to pan and cover. Cook for 2½ hours or until tender.

Oakland Raiders
11 Quarterback

DAVID HUMM

TEXAS HASH

1 lb. ground beef
1 onion, chopped
1 green pepper, chopped
1—1 lb. 12 oz. can Hunt's whole tomatoes
1 teas. chili powder
1½ teas. salt
1 teas. worcestershire sauce
¾ cup raw regular rice

Brown meat in skillet. Add onion and green pepper. Cook till tender. Drain fat. Add tomatoes and seasoning, bring to a boil. Stir in rice. Simmer 30—35 minutes. Serves 4—6. Serve with crisp salad and French bread.

•   •   •

Houston Oilers
Linebacker &
Special Teams Coach

JOHN PAUL YOUNG

JUAN PABLO'S CHILIE CON QUESO

1 lb. ground beef
½ lb. hot sausage
2 lbs. Velveeta cheese
½ lb. grated Monterey Jack cheese
1 onion, chopped
4 pickled jalapeno chiles or chopped green chiles

Cook ground beef and sausage together. Drain well. Add to cheese that has been melted in double boiler. Add onion and jalapenos. Serve hot.

RALPH PERRETTA

San Diego Chargers
53 Offensive Center

LASAGNA ALA JOANNE

2½ lb. ground beef
1 cup chopped onion
2 cloves minced garlic
1 16 oz. can tomatoes
1 16 oz. can tomato sauce

2 T. parsley flakes
2 T. sugar
1 teas. salt
1 teas. basil leaves
1 teas. Italian seasoning

•   •   •

2 12 oz. cartons ricotta cheese
½ cup parmesan cheese
2 beaten eggs (opt.)

1 T. parsley flakes
1½ teas. salt
1 teas. oregano

•   •   •

1 pkg. (8 oz.) lasagna noodles—cooked and drained
1 lb. shredded mozzarella cheese
¾ cup grated parmesan cheese

•   •   •

Cook and stir beef, onion and garlic until tender. Drain excess fat. Add tomatoes and break up with fork. Add tomato sauce, 2 T. parsley flakes, sugar and 1 teas. salt, basil and Italian seasoning.

Heat oven to 350°. Mix ricotta cheese, ½ cup parmesan cheese, 1 T. parsley, 1½ teas. salt, oregano and eggs (opt.). Reserve ¾ cup meat sauce for thin top layer.

In ungreased 13x9x2 inch pan, layer ¼ each of noodles, meat sauce, mozzarella cheese and ricotta cheese mixture, repeat 3 times. Spread reserved meat sauce over top, sprinkle parmesan cheese. (It can be covered and refrigerated for several hours or overnight).

Bake, uncovered 45 minutes (allow an extra 5 minutes if refrigerated). Enjoy!

Denver Broncos   **RED MILLER**
Head Coach

FAVORITE LASAGNA

This dish may be frozen, thawed, then baked.

> *6 T. butter or margarine*
> *1/2 cup chopped onions*
> *1 1/2 teas. garlic salad dressing mix*
> *2 cans (2 lbs. 3 oz. each) Italian tomatoes*
> *1 lb. ground beef chuck*
> *1/2 cup dry bread crumbs*
> *1/4 cup milk*
> *2 slightly beaten eggs*
> *1 cup grated Romano or Parmesan cheese*
> *1/2 cup finely chopped parsley*
> *2 1/2 T. salt*
> *1/4 teas. pepper*
> *2 cans (6 oz. each) tomato paste*
> *3 cups water*
> *1 T. sugar*
> *1 teas. fennel seed*
> *1 1/2 teas. dried basil*
> *1 lb. lasagna noodles, cooked*
> *1 lb. mozzarella cheese, thinly sliced*
> *1 lb. ricotta (Italian pot cheese) or small curd cottage cheese*

Melt 4 T. of the butter in a large saucepan. Add onions, salad dressing mix, and tomatoes. Simmer and stir until liquid has evaporated.

Meanwhile, combine beef, bread crumbs, milk, eggs, 1/4 cup of the grated Romano cheese, 1/4 cup of the chopped parsley, 1 1/2 teaspoons of the salt, and the pepper. Mix well. Brown in remaining butter in skillet.

Add meat to tomatoes. Mix in the tomato paste, water, sugar, remaining 1/4 cup chopped parsley, the fennel seed, basil, 1/4 cup grated Romano cheese, and remaining 2 T. salt. Simmer 45 minutes to 1 hour.

Pour 1 cup of the sauce into a 15x10x2 inch baking pan. Cover with a layer of drained noodles, one-third of the mozzarella cheese, one-third of the ricotta, and 2 T. of the grated cheese. Cover with sauce. Repeat with two more layers of each, ending with sauce. Sprinkle with remaining grated cheese. Bake in moderate oven (350°) for 30 minutes. Cut into squares. Serves 10 to 12.

BURTON LAWLESS

Dallas Cowboys
66 Offensive Guard

COWBOY LASAGNE

3 cups sm. sliced tomatoes	1 sm. pkg. lasagne noodles
1 pkg. spaghetti sauce mix	3 cloves crushed garlic
2 T. seasoned salt	1 teas. pepper
½ cup chopped onion (if desired)	1½ lbs. ground beef
1 cup ricotta cheese	2 cups mozzarella cheese
½ cup parmesan cheese	2 teas. oregano
1—8 oz. can tomato paste	

Brown the meat with garlic, onion, seasoned salt, pepper for 10 minutes. Add spaghetti sauce mix with recommended amount of water on package. Add tomatoes, tomato paste also. Simmer 30 minutes. Meanwhile, cook the noodles according to package directions. Add 2 T. oil to keep them from sticking and breaking. Take 8x8 inch baking dish and pour about a cup of sauce in. Make a layer of noodles, then a layer of sauce, ricotta, mozzarella, parmesan. Repeat with noodles, sauce, ricotta, etc. The last layer should not be covered with noodles. Instead sprinkle the oregano on top of the parmesan. Bake in 350° oven for 20 minutes.

* * *

DON DUFEK

Seattle Seahawks
25 Defensive Back

IRISH LASAGNE

1—8 oz. pkg. noodles	1 cup cottage cheese
1½ lbs. hamburger	¼ cup sour cream
2—8 oz. cans tomato sauce	2 T. green pepper, ⅓ cup onions
1—8 oz. pkg. cream cheese	2 T. melted butter

Cook noodles until tender. Drain. Brown hamburger in skillet, stir in tomato sauce. Remove from heat. Combine cottage cheese and cream cheese and sour cream. Add onions and green peppers. In a greased 2 qt. casserole place alternate layers of noodles, cheese mixture, noodles and hamburger mixture on top. Bake at 325° for 25—35 minutes.

Minnesota Vikings
Defensive Coordinator
Assistant Coach

BOB HOLLWAY

EASY LASAGNA

2 T. salad oil
1 lb. hamburger
2 cloves garlic, crushed
1 8 oz. can tomato sauce

1 #2 can tomatoes
1½ teas. salt
¼ teas. pepper
½ teas. oregano

Saute oil, hamburger, and garlic. Add remaining ingredients and simmer for 20 minutes until thickened slightly. Meanwhile, cook 8 oz. lasagna noodles, drain and rinse. Arrange in rectangular casserole alternate layers of:

noodles
sliced mozzarella cheese (½ lb.)
swiss cheese (½ lb.)
tomato meat sauce
grated parmesan cheese (½ cup)

ending with layer of sauce and parmesan. Bake 375° for 20 minutes.

* * *

Seattle Seahawks
60 Offensive Guard

RON CODER

MEATBALLS AND MASHED POTATOES

1 lb. hamburger
3—4 slices of white bread (slightly wet)

salt and pepper

Mix together and roll into balls (slightly flattened) the size of golf balls. Brown in skillet in 1—2 T. of hot fat. Turn and brown other side. Cook through for about 20 minutes. Remove from skillet to bowl. Empty excess oil but keep some in skillet. Remove from heat. Stir in about 2 T. of flour and don't let it get lumpy. It should be smooth. Put back on burner and add hot water (1 cup) slowly and stir. Let boil stirring constantly. When thick enough to your liking, pour meatballs back in and turn in the gravy. Heat should be low now. Make mashed potatoes.

CHRIS BAHR

Cincinnati Bengals
10 Field Goal Kicker

MEATLOAF CHEESE ROLL-UP

Great! P.A.S.S. 4—6 servings.

½ cup of sliced mushrooms	1 teas. parsley
1 lb. ground beef	½ teas. oregano
¼ cup milk	½ teas. basil
½ cup dry bread crumbs	½ teas. thyme
1 egg	2 T. fine bread crumbs
1 minced garlic clove	1 onion, diced
½ teas. salt	1 cup mozzarella cheese,
½ teas. pepper	coarsely grated
4 strips of bacon	1—16 oz. can tomato sauce

In a bowl combine beef, ½ cup bread crumbs, egg, ¼ cup of milk, salt and pepper. Mix thoroughly. Heat oven to 350°. Fry bacon—crumble and reserve bacon fat. On wax paper pat meat flat into a rectangle. Drizzle some bacon fat over meat. Sprinkle meat with parsley, oregano, basil, thyme, and 2 T. of bread crumbs. Leaving a ½ inch border scatter bacon, onion, garlic, mushrooms, and cheese over meat. Roll meat up like a jelly roll, pressing meat to contain filling. Place meat seam down in a pan and pour tomato sauce over it. Cover dish with foil and bake 50 to 60 minutes.

• • •

STEVE LUKE

Green Bay Packers
46 Safety

MEATLOAF

Ground beef with crumbled saltine or ritz crackers, green peppers, onion, eggs, oregano, bay leaf, thyme, garlic salt and pepper. Mix well and bake at 450° 1 hour 15 minutes.

ITALIAN MEAT ROLLS IN SPAGHETTI SAUCE

2—3 lb. lean sirloin steak, sliced thin and tenderized
Kraft grated parmesan cheese
1/2 to 3/4 cup chopped parsley
garlic salt and pepper
crushed red pepper (opt., use only if hot taste is desired)
1/3 cup olive oil and several T. butter

Cut steak in strips approximately 2—3 inches, sprinkle with garlic salt and pepper to taste, then sprinkle with chopped parsley, grated cheese and crushed red pepper if used. Roll up meat strips and fasten with toothpicks. Brown meat-rolls in oil and butter on both sides, and set aside in platter, to be cooked in sauce below:

• • •

ITALIAN MEAT SAUCE

1/2 lb. mushrooms   *1 cup chopped onions*
3 cloves minced garlic   *2—3 T. parsley*
small pinch of herbs   *2 jars Ragu sauce w/mushrooms*
5—6 small cans Contadina tomato sauce

In same skillet used for browning meat-rolls, brown the first 5 ingredients until tender. In the meanwhile, start Ragu sauce and tomato sauce simmering in Dutch oven, rinsing jars with small amount of water and rinsing cans of tomato sauce also with approximately 1/4 can water and adding to sauce. Add all of browned ingredients to sauce and simmer slowly for about 1 hour. Then add the browned meat rolls and cook slowly for about 1 hour or until tender. Serve over hot spaghetti or macaroni.

CHARLEY HANNAH

Tampa Bay Buccaneers
73 Defensive End or
Offensive Tackle

BEEF MUSHROOM CREPES & WINE SAUCE

These are delicious! The crepes are the time-consuming part of this recipe — the rest (meat and sauce) is quick and easy. Keep crepes made up and frozen in freezer, and this is an easy recipe to fix.

8 crepes
1¼ pounds steak (top sirloin, New York strip, filet) ¾ inch
4 T. butter   *thick*
⅓ cup minced green onion
¼ pound mushrooms (sliced)
½ cup dry white wine
¾ teas. salt
½ cup whipping cream
1½ teas. cornstarch

Use just a basic main-dish crepe recipe. Remove fat from steak; cut meat into cubes and brown in fry pan in 2 T. butter until brown and done to your preference. Spoon meat (leaving liquid in pan) from pan and keep warm. Add remaining 2 T. butter; stir in mushrooms and green onion. Cook slowly for two minutes. Stir in wine and bring to a boil. Reduce heat and simmer for 4 minutes. Remove from heat. Combine cream and corn starch; stir into sauce in pan. Cook, stirring, about 3 minutes or until thick. Spoon warm meat onto crepe, and add a little sauce, fold up sides to form a roll; top with more sauce and mushrooms. Makes 4 servings.

•   •   •

BOOKER T. BROWN

Tampa Bay Bucanneers
66 Offensive Guard

SMOTHERED CUBE STEAK

Cut up 2 T-bone steaks into cubes. Saute in worcestershire. Add onions, bell pepper, tomatoes, and mushrooms. Smother about 35 minutes on medium heat. Serve over your favorite rice. Season according to your own taste. I recommend Accent, and seasoning salt. Keep in mind the vegetables have their own seasoning so you will not need that much seasoning added.

PETE BANASZAK

RIBS AND SAUERKRAUT

One of Peter's favorite dishes. I got the recipe from his mother. Sue.

4 lbs. beef spareribs (approx.)
1 lb. can sauerkraut
¼ cup barley

Cut ribs into serving pieces, place in a slow cooker and cover with water. Salt and Pepper. Cook on low, very slow for 4—5 hours. About 1 hour before serving: drain sauerkraut, rinse and squeeze out under cold water. Pour off about half the liquid from the ribs. Bones should be falling off and can be removed. Add sauerkraut and barley. Cook till barley is soft. Serves 4-6.

* * *

New York Giants
20 Back

LELAND SHAFFER

ROLADEN—GERMAN STYLE

6 thin slices round steak (ask for Roladen cut)
1 large tomato, sliced
2 med. sized onions, finely chopped
2 slices bacon, cut into strips 3 x ½
mustard, pepper, salt, cayenne pepper

Spread mustard thinly over entire steak. Season to taste with pepper and salt. Sprinkle cayenne pepper lightly. At one end, place 1 thin slice of tomato, top with mound of chopped onions, crisscross with bacon strips. Roll up and fasten with toothpick. Place in heavy skillet with melted butter and brown well over medium heat. Cover tightly and simmer slowly on low heat for an hour or so. Baste often (it makes its own juice). Remove meat from pan while making gravy. Delicious with potato pancakes or mashed potatoes.

DOUG FRANCE

Los Angeles Rams
77 Offensive Tackle

SAUERBRATEN

4 lbs. round bone roast beef
bacon, garlic, salt, pepper
sour cream, 1—2 cups

2 cups vinegar
2 cups water
1 cup sliced onion
4 bay leaves
2 teas. peppercorns
½ cup sugar

Heat but not boil last 6 ingredients. Pour over meat and marinate 7—10 days. Turn each day until ready to cook. Cook meat until tender. Make gravy and add sour cream.

•   •   •

PETE WOODS

San Francisco
15 Quarterback

BAKED BEEF STEW

This is a one-dish meal that leaves you time to entertain while it cooks. Easy to do, and gives a non-chef a gourmet reputation.

1 lb. boneless beef stew
½ cup celery—cut in large pieces
½ cup onions—diced
1½ T. salt—dash of pepper
3 T. quick tapioca
4 med. potatoes cut in half or quarters
6—8 carrots—diced
1 cup water
1 cup wine
¾ to 1 lb. sliced raw mushrooms (or 1 large can)

Mix in a covered casserole. Bake 3½ hours at 300 degrees. DO NOT raise lid while cooking.

Alumni
Cleveland Browns
86 End

DANTE LAVELLI

5 HOUR STEW OR POT ROAST

This is great if you are going out for the afternoon!

> *2—3 lbs. stew meat or a pot roast*
> *1 can cream of celery or mushroom soup*
> *1 can tomato soup*
> *1 pkg. frozen peas*
> *2 onions*
> *carrots and potatoes*
> *seasoning—salt, pepper, garlic salt and bay leaves*

Cover tightly. Put in 250° oven for 5 hours.

• • •

Atlanta Falcons
57 Center

JEFF VAN NOTE

STEAK AUPOIVRE
(Pepper Steak)

> *4 club or strip steaks (12 oz. each) about ¾ in. thick*
> *4 T. butter*
> *2 T. peppercorns*
> *3 T. warm cognac*
> *salt to taste*
> *3 shallots, finely chopped*
> *1 cup brown sauce or canned beef gravy*

Dry steaks with paper towels. Crush peppercorns, and with the heel of your hand, rub pepper into both sides of steak. Heat 3 T. butter in large skillet. Saute steaks quickly, about 3 minutes on each side for medium rare; slightly longer, lowering heat for well done. Pour warm cognac over steaks, stand back and ignite. When the flame subsides, remove steaks, scrape off excess pepper, season with salt and place on a warm platter. Saute shallots in fat in skillet until tender. Add broth, or drippings. Cook until almost dry. Add brown sauce, bring to a boil and cook 1—2 minutes. Swirl in remaining butter. Serve separately.

CHET FRANKLIN

New Orlean Saints
Assistant Coach—Defensive Backs

ZUCCHINI STEAK

This is a nice dish for entertaining because the meat can be done very early in the day. Then later the zucchini can be added for cooking while the rice is prepared just before serving.

1 lb. seasoned round steak, cut into thin strips
3 T. cooking oil
1 10½ oz. can mushroom gravy
½ cup water—add more if sauce becomes thick
½ envelope spaghetti sauce mix with mushrooms
2—3 medium zucchini, cut into ½ inch slices
enough hot cooked rice for 4 servings

In a skillet, quickly brown strips in hot oil. Add gravy, sauce mix, and water. Cover, cook over low heat for 20 minutes, stirring occasionally. Add zucchini. Cover and continue cooking 12—15 minutes or till zucchini is tender. Serve over the hot rice. (Make sure there is adequate sauce because it is really good with the rice.)

• • •

DAVID POSEY

New England Patriots
9 Kicker

BEEF STROGANOFF

1 lb. beef	*½ cup chopped onions*
1 garlic clove	*3 teas. lemon juice*
½ pt. sour cream	*2—3 oz. cans mushrooms*
1 can consomme	*3 T. burgundy*

Brown onions, garlic and mushrooms. Add beef and brown. Add wine and lemon juice. Simmer uncovered 15 minutes. Add ¼ lb. uncooked wide noodles on top. Cover and cook until noodles are tender. Just before serving add 1 cup sour cream. Serves 4 or 5.

JOE BUGEL

MOE'S BEEF STROGANOFF

3 lbs. beef tenderloin cut in 1 x 2 inch pieces
⅓ cup dill pickles cut into strips
1 cup sour cream
1½ cups brown gravy
salt and pepper
1 teas. chopped parsley
¼ cup butter
2 T. chopped shallots or green onions

Saute beef in butter until brown. Add shallots or onions to beef and cook until clear. Season with salt and pepper. Remove beef from pan. Add brown gravy, bring to boil. Add pickles and sour cream to the sauce. Return beef to sauce and simmer for two to three minutes. Serve with noodles. Mushrooms sauted in butter may be added when pickles and sour cream are added to gravy. Serves 4—6.

*   *   *

New York Jets
Offensive Line Coach

BOB FRY

STUFFED PEPPERS

1 lb. ground beef   *½ cup cooked rice*
¼ cup chopped celery   *1 egg*
small onion, chopped   *½ can 8 oz. tomato sauce*
1 T. worcestershire sauce   *salt and pepper (to taste)*
small grated carrot   *bell peppers (seeded)*

Mix above ingredients except peppers. Stuff mixture into peppers.* Bake in 450° oven for 10 minutes, turn heat to 350° and bake 1 hour and 20 minutes.

*Add remaining tomato sauce to pan. I usually make a gravy with this with either a flour or corn starch thickener.

JEFF WEST

San Diego Chargers
80 Punter

STUFFED CABBAGE

large head of cabbage
1 lb. ground chuck
½ cup raw rice
1 grated onion, small
2 eggs
1 teas. salt
¼ teas. pepper

1 sliced raw onion
2—8 oz. cans tomato sauce
2—2½ cans whole tomatoes
juice of 2 lemons
1 teas. salt
¼ teas. pepper
½—1 cup brown sugar

Remove 12 large leaves from cabbage, trim off thick part of each leaf. Let boiling water stand on leaves a few minutes so they become easy to roll. Preheat oven 375°, combine meat, rice, grated onion, eggs, 1 teas. salt and ¼ teas. pepper. Place mound of meat mixture in cup part of each leaf. Loosely fold over sides of each leaf. Roll up. In bottom of Dutch oven place a few remaining cabbage leaves. Arrange layers of stuffed cabbage, (seam side down) and sliced onion in Dutch oven. Put tomato sauce, tomatoes, lemon juice over all. Add 1 teas. salt, ¼ teas. pepper. Bring to a boil on top of range. Sprinkle with sugar to taste. Bake covered, 1 hour; uncover; bake 2 hours.

•   •   •

RICHARD JAURON

Cincinnati Bengals
30 Safety

CHICKEN A LA JAURON

Chicken breasts (split)—brown in frying pan. Slice 1 onion and place in frying pan. Place chicken on onions. Add 1 cup boiling beef bouillon and just about any vegetables you want (carrots, etc.) Add mushrooms and sliced potato. Let simmer for 45 minutes to an hour and eat an entire meal in one pan.

Green Bay Packers
33 Fullback

BARTY SMITH

CHICKEN ALMONDINE

4—6 boneless, skinned chicken breasts
2 cans cream of mushroom soup
2/3 cup milk
slivered almonds
salt and pepper

Preheat oven 350°. Brush melted butter on one side of chicken breasts. Sprinkle with salt and pepper. Cook 20 minutes. Turn chicken, and brush with butter, salt and pepper. Cook 20 more minutes.

In a bowl, mix soup and milk. Pour over chicken and cook 20 minutes, basting occasionally. Sprinkle almonds over chicken the last 5 minutes. Serve with rice. Recipe can be doubled.

• • •

New York Giants
13 Punter

DAVE JENNINGS

BAKED CHICKEN

Takes about an hour to an hour and a half, depending upon how big the chicken is. This recipe can be used for parts or for split broilers.

Place chicken on broiler pan, skin side down. Baste evenly with melted margarine. Sprinkle on season-salt (McCormick is my favorite), paprika and black pepper. Depending upon how hot your oven is, cook for ½ hour at 325°—350° (thick pieces or broilers 35—40 minutes). Turn over and repeat process for skin side of chicken. If you like skin crispy, broil for last 5 minutes, or until skin is how you like it.

NOTES: 1. Sometime, when cooking chicken skin side down, skin has a tendency to stick to pan. When you turn over, skin tears, and you lose valuable juices that keep chicken moist. To alleviate this situation, periodically shake chicken, or salt skin lightly before placing on pan. 2. If cooked at a higher temperature, chicken has a tendency to be dry. There's nothing worse than dry chicken. That's why I cook slowly at 325°.

BUCKY DILTS

Denver Broncos
10 Punter

BIG BUCK'S CHICKEN CASSEROLE

serving dish—9 x 11—one dish will serve 6 to 8 people
2 boxes of chicken flavored rice or 2 boxes of Rice-O-Roni
medium amount of assorted chicken thighs, wings, etc.
2 cans of B&B mushrooms
2 cans cream of mushroom soup
1 lb. sausage
1 bottle worcestershire sauce
small parmesan cheese

Boil all chicken and skin chicken. Be sure and cut into bite-size pieces. Cook and drain sausage. Cook rice. Get large mixing bowl and add mushroom soup, mushrooms, rice, sausage, reasonable amount of chicken. Sprinkle occasionally with worcestershire sauce. Stir all together and put in chafing dish. Sprinkle the parmesan cheese all over top. Now all you have to do is heat and serve.

Other items with meal: brown and serve rolls, broccoli with butter and lemon sauce poured on top, bottle of white wine.

*　　*　　*

BILLY SHIELDS

San Diego Chargers
66 Offensive Tackle

CHICKEN CASSEROLE

1 pkg. chipped beef　　　　　*1/2 pt. sour cream*
6—8 chicken breast fillets　　*1/2 can water*
1 can cream of mushroom soup　*6—8 slices bacon*

Line pam sprayed casserole with chipped beef. Place chicken fillets wrapped in bacon in dish, without overlapping. Mix 1 can cream of mushroom soup and 1/2 can water with sour cream. Blend well. Pour over chicken. Bake, uncovered, in oven for 3 hours at 300° or 1 hour at 400°.

New Orleans Saints
58 Middle Linebacker

JOE FEDERSPIEL

HAM AND CHICKEN CASSEROLE

*2 cups cooked ham or chicken
  or a mixture of the two
1 cup sliced celery
1 medium onion chopped fine
1½ cups cooked rice
1 can cream of mushroom soup*

*½ teas. salt
1 T. lemon juice
¾ cup mayonnaise
¼ cup water
3 hard cooked eggs, sliced*

Combine all ingredients the day before. Refrigerate overnight. Top with buttered crumbs. Bake 400° for 45 minutes. Serves 4—6.

* * *

Green Bay Packers
68 Offensive Tackle

GREG KOCH

KING'S RANCH CASSEROLE

1 lg. hen or 2 fryers (stewed with salt, pepper, onion, carrot & celery)

After chicken is cooked, remove from bone and either cut or tear into bite sized pieces.

*12 soft tortillas
1 onion, chopped
2 cups grated cheddar cheese
  (either plain or sharp)*

*1 can cream of mushroom soup
1 can cream of chicken soup
½ soup can chicken broth
½ can Rotel tomatoes*

Mix soups, broth and tomatoes together. Layer as follows in 3 qt. oblong casserole:

> chicken
> tortillas (cut in strips of 3)
> onion
> cheese
> sauce

Makes 2 layers of each. Top with ⅓ of the cheese. Bake at 325° for one hour.

JIM KIICK

Alumni
Miami Dolphins
21 Running Back

CHICKEN CORDON BLEAU

20 minutes to prepare, 40 minutes to bake.

4 whole chicken breasts (boned, halved, skinned)
8-3 inch slices boiled ham
8-2 x 2 pieces of gruyere cheese (1 oz.)
1 stick of butter
1 cup of fresh bread crumbs
1 teas. of salt
¼ teas. of paprika

Pull each half breast open in middle to form a pocket. Fold ham around cheese. Tuck into the pocket. Melt butter. Make fresh bread crumbs in a blender. Mix bread crumbs with salt and paprika. Roll stuffed chicken breasts in melted butter, then in bread crumb mixture. Place in buttered baking dish and bake, 400° for 40 minutes or until brown.

•   •   •

LYLE BLACKWOOD

Baltimore Colts
44 Free Safety

CHICKEN ENCHILADAS

1 can green chilis   *1 onion*
1 can cream of mushroom soup   *1 can cream of chicken soup*
1 can pet milk   *1 chicken fryer*
tortillas   *cheddar cheese*

Boil chicken. Dice onions and saute in 1 T. of butter. Drain green chilis, dice and add to onions. Stir in cream of mushroom, cream of chicken, and pet milk. Add 1 cup of the chicken broth. Shred chicken and add to the mixture. In greased 13x9 pan, in order: 1 layer of tortillas, grated cheddar cheese, chicken mixture. Repeat and top with cheddar cheese. Bake at 350° for 30 minutes.

82—Souper Bowl of Recipes

Alumni
Philadelphia Eagles
53 Center

KENNETH D. FARRAGUT

CHICKEN DIVAN

Not only good, it's pretty.

> 2 pkg. frozen brocolli spears, cooked
>   or use fresh (about a pound or so)
> 8 boneless chicken breast slices, cooked
> 8 slices of ham
> 1 can cream of chicken soup
> ½ cup Kraft mayonnaise
> 1 T. lemon juice
> ½ cup of whipping cream, whipped
> 1-4 oz. cheddar cheese, grated
> 1 jar of pimento strips

Place brocolli in greased casserole (3 qt.). Top with ham, chicken. Blend in pot, soup, mayonnaise, and lemon juice. Fold in whipped cream. Pour on top and top with cheddar cheese and pimento strips. Bake 350° for 30—45 minutes.

•   •   •

Philadelphia Eagles
Defensive Co-Ordinator

MARION CAMPBELL

CURRIED CHICKEN DIVAN

1 pack minute rice	1 cup of mayonnaise
4 deboned chicken breasts	½ teas. of curry powder
1 teas. of lemon juice	½ cup of bread crumbs
1 cup of shredded cheddar cheese	2 T. melted butter
2-10 oz. pkgs. frozen broccoli	2 cans cream of chicken soup

Boil rice. Pre-cook chicken, place in bowl. Pre-cook broccoli, place in bowl. Spread broccoli in casserole dish. Place chicken on top. In a separate bowl combine soup, mayonnaise, lemon juice and curry powder. Pour on chicken. Sprinkle bread crumbs on top. Bake at 350° for 25 minutes and serve over rice.

KAY STEPHENSON

Buffalo Bills
Quarterback Coach

MEXICAN CHICKEN

7—8 chicken breasts—boiled, deboned, and torn in pieces
1 lb. Montery Jack or cheddar cheese, grated
1 can enchilada sauce
1 can cream of chicken soup
1 pkg. frozen tortillas, thawed and sliced in strips
2 small bell peppers, chopped
2 small onions chopped
2 T. butter

Saute peppers and onions in butter. Mix 1 can enchilada sauce with ¾ can chicken soup in blender. Add 1 T. garlic powder and 1 T. chili powder. Dash salt and pepper. In greased casserole (I use 9x13 pyrex), place ½ of cut up chicken, sprinkle with ½ the peppers and onions, cover with a layer of sliced tortillas. Pour enough sauce mixture to moisten well. Sprinkle with ½ the cheese. Repeat layers ending with cheese. Line the sides of the pan with remaining tortillas. (You may have a little sauce left over.) Bake at 350° for 35 to 40 minutes. Serves 6.

* * *

HENRY LAWRENCE

Oakland Raiders
70 Offensive Tackle

FRIED TO STEWED CHICKEN

Cut and prepare chicken. Season with milk and beat eggs (season). Put flour in bag and put seasoning in it.

garlic salt	*pinch of red pepper*
seasoned salt	*meat tenderizer*
black pepper	*any other seasoning desired*

Put chicken in milk and eggs. Soak chicken. Place in bag of seasoned flour, shake well. Cook normal. (I use cover to keep the flavor in the pan in order to be absorbed by the chicken, better flavor.) Also good stewed after you've fried it. Can be baked or broiled.

New England Patriots
32 Running Back

ANDY JOHNSON

CHICKEN KIEV

This is a sophisticated "Fried Chicken" with an unusual flavor because of the tarragon spice. It can be made in advance, frozen, deep fried before serving and still warm in the oven if the dinner is delayed. Good after the game.

3-12—14 oz. chicken breasts　　*2 eggs beaten lightly*
salt & pepper to taste　　*3 T. milk, may need more*
1 1/4 cup softened butter　　*1/3 cup flour*
2 T. tarragon　　*1 cup fine dry bread crumbs*
1 T. parsley

Bone and halve chicken breasts. Place each piece of chicken between wax paper and pound to 1/4 inch thick. Mix butter, tarragon, salt and pepper, parsley together—place it on a piece of aluminum foil and put into freezer until firm enough to cut into squares. Put 1 butter square in the center of each piece of chicken. Tuck in short ends; fold long ends over and secure with a wooden toothpick. Mix eggs and milk. Roll chicken in flour; dip in egg mixture. Roll in bread crumbs. Dip in egg and roll in bread crumbs again. Deep fry the chicken about 14 minutes or until golden brown. Then bake for 10 minutes at 500°. Gently remove picks and melt any remaining butter to serve as a sauce.

*　　*　　*

Green Bay Packers
Wide Receiver

REGGIE CRAIG

GRANNY KERR'S CHICKEN AND DUMPLINGS

Cook chicken in a lot of water. Salt and pepper (1 hour). Cool—debone chicken. Set aside.

Dumplings: Mix 2 cups flour, 1 teas. salt and 1/4 teas. baking powder. Add 2 T. shortening and mash up. Then 2/3 — 3/4 cup broth from chicken. (Should be like pie dough.) Take half and roll out thin on floured paper. Cut in little long strips. Drop one at a time in hot chicken broth. Do other half the same way. Cook on medium until done with lid on. Add chicken. Don't stir much, but it does stick so watch it.

BILL BERGEY

Philadelphia Eagles
66 Inside Linebacker

SPANISH PAELLA

¼ cup all purpose flour
1 teas. salt
1-2½—3 lb. ready to cook
broiler-fryer chicken, cut up
¼ cup of olive or salad oil
2 carrots, pared & sliced lengthwise
2 med. onions, quartered
1 celery branch with leaves
2 cups chicken broth
1 clove garlic, crushed

¼ cup diced canned pimento
½ teas. salt
¼ teas. ground oregano
¼ teas. ground saffron
⅔ cup uncooked, long-
grained rice
1-9 oz. pkg. frozen
artichoke hearts,
thawed (opt.)
¾ lb. shelled raw shrimp
12 small clams in shell

Combine flour, 1 teas. salt, and dash pepper in plastic or paper bag. Add a few chicken pieces at a time; shake to coat. In heavy skillet, brown chicken in hot oil about 20 minutes. Transfer to large kettle. Add next 10 ingredients; simmer covered for 30 minutes. Add artichoke hearts, shrimp, and clams in shells; simmer covered for 15—20 minutes longer. (Until clams are steamed and open.) Serves 6—8 people.

*   *   *

LOU GROZA

Hall of Fame
Cleveland Browns
76 Tackle & Place Kicker

CHICKEN WITH SWISS CHEESE & STUFFING

boned chicken breasts
2 cans cream of chicken soup

swiss cheese slices
1 pkg. Pepperidge Farm stuffing

Butter 9x13 pan (I use pyrex). Cut boned and skinned breasts in half. Place in pan. Cover each piece with slice of Swiss cheese. Cover with chicken soup—undiluted. Cover with foil and bake at 350° for 45 minutes, making stuffing as directed. Spread on top of casserole and bake 10 minutes longer. Serve immediately.

Pittsburgh Steelers
65 Defensive Line

TOM BEASLEY

CHICKEN PIE

2 cooked, cubed chickens
1 can cream of celery soup
1 can water
small minced green pepper
3 or 4 cans of flakey biscuits
1 small minced onion
1 small can peas (drain)
1 small can carrots (drain)
salt and pepper to taste

Mix all ingredients (except biscuits). Line bottom of buttered casserole dish with divided layers of biscuits. Pour chicken mixture on top of biscuits and top with divided layers of biscuits. Bake at 350° until casserole starts bubbling; increase temperature to 425° until biscuits brown.

•   •   •

Alumni
San Francisco Forty Niners
NBC Sportscaster

JOHN BRODIE

TERIYAKI CHICKEN

½ cup soy sauce
1 clove garlic
fresh ginger (½ T. grated)

½ cup brown sugar
¼ cup sake (rice wine)

Mix above ingredients and bring to a boil. Boil about 1 minute, remove from heat and cool slightly. Pour mixture over 2—3 pound chicken, (cut-up). Marinate at least 2 hours. Bake in oven until chicken is tender. Delicious served hot or cold.

CRAIG COLQUITT

Pittsburgh Steelers
5 Kicking Specialist

CORNISH GAME HENS

1 pkg. long grain wild rice
pepper
salt
butter

Preheat oven to 325°. Salt and pepper birds cavities. Cook 1 hour fifteen minutes. Should have rice cooked when birds are finished. Stuff rice into bird cavities and serve with a green vegetable, salad and Bouchard Pere & Fils Pouilly-Fuisse or your favorite dry wine. And one of your favorite persons.

•   •   •

CHARLEY WINNER

Cincinnati Bengals
Assistant Coach

CORNISH HEN IN WINE

cornish hens	*thyme*
butter	*garlic clove, split*
salt	*chicken stock or consomme*
pepper	*½ cup white wine*
paprika	*sauteed mushrooms*
lemon juice	*white grapes*
worcestershire	*chopped ripe olives or truffles*
tabasco	*¼ cup white wine*

Rub each hen with butter, salt, pepper, lemon juice, worcestershire, tabasco, thyme and split garlic clove. Place in roaster with about one inch of stock or consomme, bake covered in 275° oven for two to two and a half hours. When half done, add one half cup white wine. About a half hour before removing from oven, add mushrooms, grapes, olives or truffles and additional wine. If more liquid is needed during cooking, add wine. Remove cover before cooking time is complete to speed cooking and also to brown hens.

Green Bay Packers
17 Quarterback

DAVID WHITEHURST

CORN BREAD DRESSING
(Chicken or Turkey)

Egg bread	*1 teas. salt*
1½ cups cornmeal	*5 T. shortening, bacon drippings*
½ cup flour	*1 cup buttermilk*
2 teas. baking powder	*2 eggs*
6—8 slices dry toast (crumbled)	
¾ cup cooked rice (can be left-over)	
1½ cup finely chopped celery	
1 cup finely cut onions	

Mix well all ingredients except toast, rice, celery and onions—add more milk if needed, pour into a greased skillet or bread pan. Bake at 425° for 30 minutes, or until brown. Let cool. Break bread into large mixing bowl. Add remaining ingredients. Moisten with stock from chicken, turkey or pork (approximately 2 qts). Canned chicken broth may be used. Add 3 raw eggs, salt, pepper and poultry seasoning to taste. Stir well. Add more stock if necessary until mixture is thin. If stock is not rich enough, add butter as desired. If too greasy, add water. Bake at 425° for 30 to 40 minutes or until brown.

* * *

Baltimore Colts
Head Trainer Emeritus

EDWARD BLOCK

TIJUANA DRESSING

Dice into ¼ inch pieces, pepperoni, salami, garlic bologna, hot sausage, tuna or 3 other types of lunch meat or sausage, to taste. Dice thick sliced bacon into ¼ inch pieces and fry. Use at least ½ lb. or more to taste. Add the rest of the pieces to the frying bacon. Do not pour out the grease. Prepare a package of dressing using a can of chicken broth to wet the dry ingredients. Add the meat to the prepared dressing. Bake at 350° for about ½ hour.

DURIEL HARRIS

Miami Dolphins
82 Wide Receiver

RICE DRESSING
(Dirty Rice)

1 cup chopped onions
1 cup chopped bell peppers
1 cup chopped celery
1/2 cup chopped green onions, tops and bottoms
4 garlic cloves, chopped also
1 small bunch parsley leaves, coarsely chopped
1 lb. ground steak
1 lb. chopped chicken livers
1 lb. pork sausage
3 cups cooked rice, do not overcook

In a large skillet cook ground meat, pork sausage and chicken livers, for about 15 minutes. Add onions, bell pepper, celery, green onions and add salt and pepper to taste. Cover and let simmer for about 20 minutes. Add parsley. Fold in cooked rice. Mix well but do not mash. Serve hot. Goes very well with stuffed pork roast.

•　　•　　•

JACK YOUNGBLOOD

Los Angeles Rams
85 Defensive End

ROASTED WILD DUCK
(Better known as Camp House Duck)

I prefer the wood duck best of all but if not available, the mallard, bullneck (ringneck) will do. Take birds and salt and pepper heavily. Put ducks in roaster on a rack—put inside peeled orange slices, apple wedges and celery—around duck add carrots and new potatoes.

Fill bottom of roaster with water and red wine—right to bottom of ducks on the rack—Cook at 300° for 2½ to 3 hours. Serve on bed of brown and wild rice with vegetables on side—a good cold night's dinner along with a good red burgundy.

ELROY L. (CRAZYLEGS) HIRSCH

CRAZYLEGS LAMB

5 lb. leg of lamb
several halved garlic bulbs
salt & pepper to taste

garlic salt
dash of celery salt

Take a five pound leg of lamb and cut slits into the thicker parts of the meat and insert halved garlic bulbs. Generously season with salt, pepper, garlic salt and a dash of celery salt—do this to both sides. Place the meat in a deep pan which contains a mixture of one bottle of white wine, bay leaves and worcestershire sauce. Allow to marinate a total of 24 hours in the refrigerator, but turn the meat over after the first 12 hours. Place the meat on a hot charcoal grill and sear both sides. Then drop the fire as low as possible and proceed to cook from approximately 45 minutes to an hour (very slowly). The length of time will depend upon the thickness of the meat. After searing, generously apply barbecue sauce to the top side of the meat after each turning. This will build up a thick "crust" of barbecue sauce which greatly adds to the flavor. When the meat is done per your desire, remove from fire and slice on a bias and flick out the garlic bulbs as you come to them.

* * *

Tampa Bay
Coach—Defense

ABE GIBRON

KIBBI NAYYA
(Raw Ground Lamb with Crushed Wheat)

1½ cup fine burghul (crushed wheat)
1 lb. lean boneless lamb (preferably leg of lamb, finely ground
  3 times)
¼ teas. ground all spice & pinch of ground nutmeg
2 teas. salt, freshly ground pepper
olive oil for garnish

Place the burghyl in a bowl of cold water to cover and let it soak for 10 minutes. Squeeze dry. Add to the ground lamb with your hands, knead until the mixture is smooth. Add remaining spices and shape into a round flat cake and form a large X in the center, into the X pour the olive oil. Serve with Arab bread. Serves 8.

CARL TASEFF

Miami Dolphins
Assistant Coach

MARINATED LEG OF LAMB

1 leg of lamb, 5—6 lbs.
salt & pepper
3 garlic cloves, mashed or slivered
1 T. oregano

½ teas. thyme
juice of one lemon
½ cup olive oil
1½ cups white wine

Wash and dry the lamb, season with salt and pepper, and rub it well with mashed garlic (or place the garlic slivers in slits in the lamb.) Rub oregano and thyme on all sides of the lamb, sprinkle lemon juice, pour wine and olive oil over lamb, turn to completely coat with juices. Marinate for several hours. Roast lamb at 325°. Insert meat thermometer, careful not to touch the bone. When temperature reaches 165°F will be medium or 170°—180°F for well, taking about 3 hours, basting with marinade occasionally. (Marinated leg is particularly delicious when roasted on a spit over charcoal, again place thermometer into meat and cook until temperature 165°F medium or 170°—180°F well.) Serve with beans. Serves 6.

•   •   •

ALAN C. PAGE

Chicago Bears
82 Defensive Tackle

LEG OF LAMB

Great for entertaining!

4 cloves garlic, chopped
⅓ cup honey
½ cup boiling water

1 cup Kikkoman soy sauce
1 leg of lamb
½ cup white wine

Mix garlic, honey and boiling water, stir until honey is dissolved. Add soy sauce. Pour over lamb; marinate 4 to 8 hours turning lamb several times. Put in roasting pan and add ½ cup marinade. Cook 30 minutes per pound at 325°, adding the wine halfway through the cooking. Slice lamb across grain and pour cooking sauce over meat.

St. Louis Cardinals
Vice President—Operations

JOE SULLIVAN

LEG-O-LAMB

Have your butcher butterfly a good sized leg-o-lamb. Take one pint of sour cream (or dietetic substitute), add garlic, salt, black pepper, and optional spices to the sour cream. Completely cover the leg-o-lamb with sour cream mixture and allow to marinate for a minimum of four hours (the longer the better). Then, bar-b-que over hot coals twenty minutes on each side.

* * *

Cleveland Browns
52 Linebacker

DICK AMBROSE

BREADED PORK CHOPS & SCALLOPED POTATOES

In greased casserole dish, put in layers of:

sliced raw potatoes (4—5 medium)
sliced raw onions (one)
salt and pepper to taste

Add one can of cream of mushroom soup and ¾ can of milk. Put in 350° oven for 45 minutes. 15 minutes before potatoes are done:

1 dish cracker crumbs (saltine)
1 bowl, 2 eggs, beaten
4 to 5 pork chops

Dip chops in eggs—then cracker crumbs. Brown in frying pan with 3 T. oil. Place browned chops on top of potatoes. Cover and bake 350° oven for 45 minutes more. Total cooking time 1½ hours.

A. J. DUHE

Miami Dolphins
77 Defensive End

ANDOUILLE OR PORK JAMBALAYA

One of A. J.'s delights since he was a very little boy. Hope you enjoy it as well. Mrs. Adam Duhe (mother).

3 T. oil	*⅓ cup catsup*
1 andouille (12 oz.	*1 very lg. mild onion*
size cut in pieces	*4 cloves garlic, minced*
or 1 lb. fresh pork cut in cubes	*1 lb. ground meat (baby beef)*
⅓ cup chopped bell pepper	*2 cups long grain raw rice*
4¼ cups hot water	*2 T. chicken seasoned stock base*
2 T. worcestershire sauce	*(Spice Island)*
3 dashes tabasco sauce (opt.)	*½ teas. oregano whole leaves*
3 T. parsley	*1-8 oz. can sliced mushrooms*

In heavy bottom Dutch oven or heavy bottom chicken fryer, heat the oil (on medium heat); fry the andouille until it loses its pinkness. Remove from pan; drain off excess fat, leaving only a small amount on bottom of pot. Fry ground meat until lightly browned, remove from pan being careful to drain excess fat. Fry onions and garlic until onions are wilted. Add raw rice and fry until all grains are light toast color. Then combine ground meat and andouille with rice; add bell pepper and sliced mushrooms in pot; mix thoroughly. Add chicken seasoned stock base, catsup, worcestershire sauce, add tabasco sauce, 4¼ cups of hot water. Add to rice and meat; oregano and parsley; bring to a boil, then lower heat. Cover and simmer 40 minutes or until all the liquid is absorbed, and rice is tender. During this process you may stir at least 3 times. Remember it is the long slow cooking that gives Jambalaya its wonderful flavor.

* * *

BRAD VAN PELT

New York Giants
10 Linebacker

BREADED HAM

Cut pre-cooked ham in approximately ¼ inch thick serving portions. Dip each slice in a mixture of well beaten egg and ¼ cup of milk. Gently coat each slice with fine soda cracker crumbs. Brown each side until golden (about 3 minutes) in a fry pan (use margarine) at approximately 360°.

JOHN THOMPSON

CHALLENGE PORK CHOPS

1 inch thick pork chops
seasoned salt (see below)
2—3 T. white wine
seasoned salt:
  2 T. salt
  2 T. sugar
  2 T. monosodium glutamate
  1 T. black pepper
  1 T. dry lemon powder
  1 T. paprika (opt.)

Sprinkle both sides of pork chops with seasoned salt mixture. Grill until brown and seared on both sides, turning frequently. Pour the wine in the bottom of a heavy frying pan. Add the chops to the pan. Place pan on grill and, if using a covered barbecue, cover. If not, either cover the frying pan or wrap chops individually in foil, adding a bit of wine to each foil packet before placing directly on the grill. Steam chops about 30 minutes.

* * *

Chicago Bears
86 Punter

BOB PARSONS

HAM AND CHEESE MEATLOAF

2 beaten eggs
½ cup Ragu or any tomato sauce
½ teas. oregano
¼ teas. pepper
2 lbs. ground beef
6 oz. shredded mozzarella

¾ cup bread crumbs
2 T. parsley flakes
1 teas. salt
¼ teas. garlic powder
½ lb. sliced boiled ham

Combine eggs, bread crumbs, sauce, parsley, oregano, salt, pepper and garlic. Mix into ground beef. Lay a piece of waxed paper on the counter and pat the ground beef mixture into a rectangular shape. Arrange ham slices on the meat and sprinkle the shredded cheese on top of the ham. Roll the meat lengthwise and seal edges and ends. Place seam side down in 9x13 pan and bake 1 hour 15 minutes at 350°. When done, put sauce and more cheese on the top and put back in the oven to melt the cheese.

KIM McQUILKEN

Washington Redskins
11 Quarterback

HAM LOAF

This recipe has been handed down from my grandmother, Mrs. Hilda Bartholomew of Allentown, Pa. The ham loaf has always been reserved for special occasions (Easter, Christmas, etc.). I have enjoyed it all my life and hopefully you will now too.

HAM LOAF:
1½ lb. ground ham
1 lb. ground pork
1 egg, beaten
¾ cup bread crumbs
¾ cup milk
pepper, to taste

GLAZE:
2 teas. prepared mustard
¼ cup brown sugar, packed
vinegar, just enough
to make spreadable

Mix together ham, pork, egg, bread crumbs, milk and pepper. Shape into loaf and place in ungreased baking pan. Stir together mustard, brown sugar, and vinegar; spread over loaf. Bake in 350° oven for 2 hours.

* * *

NICK SKORICH

National Football League
Assistant Supervisor of Officials

YUGOSLAVIA HAM AND SAUERKRAUT

For a person that likes sauerkraut, this Yugoslavian dish is a meal within itself.

4 cups diced smoke ham
2 cups red beans

8 cups sauerkraut
2 cups white sauce

Cook the ham and sauerkraut over low heat for 45 minutes or until ham is well done. Add white sauce and simmer until sauce is well blended into the ham and sauerkraut juice. Last add the red beans and simmer 5 minutes longer. Serve hot. Serves 4.

San Diego Chargers
42 Strong Safety

MIKE FULLER

HAM ROLLS

Here is Mike's favorite recipe, and much to my luck it's quick and easy. This is a good way to get picky eaters to eat broccoli! Mike always requests this when we have company. Penny.

8 slices of the rectangular packaged ham slices (like Darola)
4 slices of rectangular swiss cheese slices
1 package frozen broccoli spears

SAUCE:

1 stick margarine
1 can cream chicken soup
⅓ cup lemon juice (fresh is better)
salt (just a little)
¼ teas. pepper

blend together
in saucepan
over medium heat

Cook broccoli according to package directions and drain. To make ham rolls: lay 1 slice of ham flat, top with ½ slices of cheese then a stalk of broccoli. Then roll up and secure with a toothpick. Place rolls in casserole and cover with sauce. Bake for 30 minutes at 350⁰.

• • •

Washington Redskins
Offensive Coordinator

JOE WALTON

ITALIAN SAUSAGE & PEPPERS

2 lbs. Italian sausage
5 peeled med. size potatoes, sliced
1 cup vegetable oil
2 onions sliced
2 large green peppers sliced

1 T. oregano
½ T. salt
½ teas. pepper
dash garlic salt

In oblong casserole dish, put oil, add sausage (2 inch cut pieces), spread sliced potatoes around and between sausage, on top spread onion sliced as you would onion rings. Place green pepper on top. Sprinkle salt, pepper, oregano and garlic salt. Do not cover. Place in oven at 350⁰ for 1 hour (maybe adding more oil if necessary until brown). Stir occasionally. Makes 4 to 6 servings.

JOHN WOODCOCK

Detroit Lions
77 Defensive Tackle

WOODY'S HAWAIIAN SPARERIBS

Once your family tastes these ribs, they'll want an instant replay for sure. They may also be done in foil on a barbecue and basted for that last 30 – 40 minutes.

5 lbs. spareribs
  (split & partly cut through)
1 teas. Italian seasoning
1 onion (small) chopped
¼ cup soy sauce
½ cup brown sugar

1 clove garlic, minced
¼ teas. ground ginger
½ cup pineapple juice
1 T. cornstarch
½ cup white vinegar

Cover ribs with water and add Italian seasoning and onion. Bring to a boil and simmer for one hour. Drain. Place ribs in single layer in roasting pan. Combine all the rest of the ingredients and cook until thickened. Pour over ribs and bake for 30 minutes or til brown and glazy in 350° oven.

• • •

FRED BILETNIKOFF

Oakland Raiders
25 Wide Receiver

BOUILLABAISSE

4 cups water
1 can (8 oz.) tomato sauce
½ cup finely chopped onion
1 clove garlic, finely chopped
1 teas. lemon juice
2 T. dried parsley flakes
2½ teas. salt (opt. to taste)

¼ teas. curry powder
¼ teas. pepper
1 lb. fish fillet, cut into 2" pieces
12 oz. shrimp, shelled
6 oz. crab or lobster meat
1 pt. clams

Pour water in 4 qt. glass casserole. Cover with glass lid or plastic wrap. Microwave on high for 10 minutes or until bubbly. Stir in remaining ingredients in order given. Return to oven and continue cooking on high for about 12 minutes. Stir and continue cooking on high 8—10 minutes or until seafood is done. Let stand covered 5 minutes. Tip: top with seasoned croutons. 12 Servings.

Denver Broncos
23 Defensive Back

CHRIS PANE

WEINER DISH

For a special touch add some more velveeta cheese to the top and broil it to a semi burned condition. It is quite filling so plan with a salad.

2 lbs. hot dogs
6 large baking potatoes
⅓ onion
olive chips (small can)

CHEESE SAUCE:
1 lb. Velveeta cheese
1 teas. flour
1 teas. butter
1 cup milk

Boil potatoes (peeled and chopped into bite size pieces until a fork will barely support its weight. Meanwhile, begin mixing the cheese sauce together. Melt cheese and other ingredients slowly so as to not burn it. (I learned the hard way!) Chop ⅓ onion. Cut hot dogs into bite size pieces. After potatoes have become soft enough (but not too soft) remove the water with a strainer. In a large casserole begin to layer all 5 ingredients. Start with the potatoes on the bottom and sprinkle the hotdogs, olives, onions and top with the cheese sauce. Do this 3—4 times until all the mouth watering morsels have been exhausted. Bake in oven at 375° for ½ hour.

• • •

New England Patriots
Coach—Offensive Backs

JOHN POLONCHEK

CLAM CAKES

1 egg beaten
½ cup milk
cracker crumbs (1½ pkgs.)

¼ teas. ginger
2 cups clams, well drained
(chopped and diced)

Beat together egg, milk and ginger. Add clams and crumbs so mixture is consistency of hamburger. Drop cakes into hot oil in frying pan. Turn once. Salt or pepper as desired. A favorite in Maine eaten with catsup or vinegar. (Use a minimum of oil for frying.)

DICK CONN

New England Patriots
22 Defensive Back

CRAB MEAT AU GRATIN

3 T. butter
1 lb. crabmeat
3 T. flour

1 cup milk
¼ cup cream sherry

Melt butter in heavy pot; add 3 T. flour. Grate ½ lb. cheese and put aside. Blend flour and butter and add 1/8 teas. salt and 1 cup milk slowly over medium heat. If lumps start, take off fire and stir some. Stir constantly until thickened. Add ¾ cheese and ¼ cup cream sherry plus crabmeat. Top with remaining cheese and dot with butter. Cook 45 minutes at 350⁰.

•   •   •

MIKE PHIPPS

Chicago Bears
15 Quarterback

FLIPS FISH CASSEROLE

fish fillets
potatoes, sliced thin
onions, sliced thin

tomatoes, sliced thin
salt & pepper
Velveeta cheese, sliced thick

In the bottom of a broiler pan or cookie sheet, put a piece of heavy duty foil long enough to make a tent. Butter the bottom of foil. Layer fish, potatoes, onions, tomatoes, salt, pepper and cover with cheese. Bring ends of foil up and make a tent over casserole. Crimp the sides so that it is completely enclosed. Have grill at medium to low heat. Slide foil out of pan directly onto grill. Grill about 15—20 minutes until the foil puffs up. At this point, make a slit in the top of foil so that the steam can escape. 5 more minutes and it's done. We use bass filets, of course, from Lake Okeechobee, but you can substitute your favorite fish as long as the filets aren't too thick. Pull foil tent back onto pan so that when you serve, if foil is punctured, the juices will remain in pan instead of spilling into the grill.

Alumni
Los Angeles Rams
NBC Announcer
74 Defensive Tackle

MERLIN OLSEN

MERLIN'S MAGIC FISH DINNER

2 lbs. filet of sole in bottom of pyrex casserole. Mix 2 T. sherry* and 2 T. flour to one can of shrimp soup. Pour over fish. Cook at 300° for one hour and set aside. Just prior to serving, cover with fresh sliced mushrooms and bay shrimp. Dot with butter and add pepper to taste. Cover with parmesan cheese and sprinkle with paprika. Broil for 5 minutes and serve.
*More Sherry can be used but add equal amount of flour. Serves 6.

•   •   •

Oakland Raiders
22 Running Back

ARTHUR WHITTINGTON

FISH FRY

This is also a favorite of Horace E. King, Detroit Lions, 25 Offensive Back.

Leave fish in milk and lemon juice for an hour or two. Add salt and pepper. Dip fish in corn meal and fry until crisp.

•   •   •

Seattle Seahawks
10 Quarterback

JIM ZORN

BARBECUED SALMON

I think it's excellent with fresh corn and a fresh fruit salad.

First lay open your salmon (keep the skin on, and don't worry about the bones.) Prepare the barbeque like always. Then put foil over the grill; poke holes in the foil so the smoke will come through. Lay the salmon on the foil (skin side down). It should never be turned over. Make a butter sauce with seasonings added to the melted butter. (Be creative here). Make sure the salmon is hot and cooking before applying the butter. You can either cook it slow or faster by covering the barbeque with the lid. Cook until the salmon is a light pink. The bones should lift right out and the skin should stay stuck right on the foil.

ARTHUR MODELL

Cleveland Browns
Owner

FISH PIE
(For 2)

If I can bake this, anyone can!

1 can salmon
4 large mashed potatoes
seasonings (garlic powder, dry mustard,
    oregano, parsley, cayenne, etc.)

1 cup white wine
cheddar cheese

Put salmon, drained, in casserole—cover with wine. Mix in half of potatoes, add seasonings. Cover with cheese. Top with remaining potatoes which have been seasoned with parsley, salt and pepper, butter. Pat with butter and stick in a couple of bay leaves. Bake at 350° until heated through.

* * *

FRAN POLSFOOT

Denver Broncos
Assistant Coach

SHRIMP CREOLE

3 T. olive oil
1/2 cup diced celery
1/2 cup diced onions
1 can tomatoes
1 can tomato paste, small
2 cans tomato sauce, small
1 T. sugar
1 T. chili powder

2 T. worcestershire sauce
1 teas. tabasco
1 1/2 teas. salt
1 teas. garlic salt or
1 clove crushed garlic
2 lbs. deveined shrimp
    cooked and peeled
1 cup diced bell pepper

Cook celery, onion in oil over low heat in large pan. Then add tomatoes which have been mashed fine, tomato paste, tomato sauce, sugar, chili powder, worcestershire, tabasco, salt, garlic salt or garlic—to this add the shrimp and bell pepper and simmer 45 minutes. When ready to serve, dissolve 1 T. cornstarch in water and add to thicken. Serve over rice.

Buffalo Bills
6 Place Kicker

TOM DEMPSEY

BARBEQUE SHRIMP

1 cup salt butter	½ teas. salt
1 cup vegetable oil	½ teas. cayenne (or to taste)
2 teas. finely minced garlic	1 T. paprika
4 whole bay leaves, crushed fine	¾ teas. fresh blk. pepper
½ teas. dried basil	1 teas. fresh lemon juice
½ teas. oregano	2 lbs. whole, fresh shrimp in shell
2 teas. crushed dried rosemary leaves	

In a heavy saute pan or sauce pan, melt butter, then add the oil and mix well. Add all other ingredients except shrimp and cook over medium heat, stirring constantly, until the sauce begins to boil. Reduce the heat to low and simmer for 7—8 minutes, stirring frequently, then remove the pan from heat and let stand, uncovered, at room temperature for at least 30 minutes. Add the shrimp to the sauce, mix thoroughly, and put the pan back on burner. Cook over medium heat for 6—8 minutes or just until the shrimp turns pink, then put the pan in a 450° oven and bake for 10 minutes. Serve equal portions of shrimp with about ½ cup of sauce ladled over each one. It is perfectly alright to eat this with your hands and French bread to get all the sauce. Serves 4.

•   •   •

St. Louis Cardinals
68 Guard

TERRY S. STIEVE

ETOUFEE

½ cup butter	salt and pepper
1 bunch shallots	cayenne
½ bell pepper	½ cup chicken bouillon
2 stalks celery	4 T. flour
3 lbs. peeled and deveined shrimp	parsley

Chop vegetables and saute in butter. Add shrimp, bouillon, salt, pepper and cayenne to taste. Cook until bubbly. Sprinkle flour over mixture and cover. Simmer 1 hour. Serve over rice.

Crawfish may be substituted adding 1 T. tomato paste to mixture.

ED G. BILES

Houston Oilers
Defensive Coordinator

BAKED RED SNAPPER

6 lbs. headless red snapper
1 cup minced onions
1 teas. salt
pepper to taste
lemon slices

¼ cup olive or cooking oil
2 cans chopped tomatoes
3 fresh peeled tomatoes
1 teas. minced hot peppers

Rub the snapper in and out with salt and pepper. Place in a long foil lined, baking pan and cover with minced and hot pepper. Bake in 350° oven about 45 minutes, basting with plenty of olive or cooking oil. Add can of tomatoes with juice and one can drained, plus 3 fresh tomatoes (be sure to place some inside fish). Continue baking 45 minutes more. 15 minutes before removing from oven, garnish fish with slices of fresh tomatoes and lemon.

• • •

SHANE NELSON

Buffalo Bills
59 Linebacker

TUNA AND AVOCADO SANDWICHES

1 can tuna
½ cup chopped apple
½ cup raisins

¼ cup chopped onions
3 T. mayonnaise

Season tuna with lemon juice, salt and pepper. Add apples, raisins, and onions. Mix all together with mayonnaise. Mash 1 large avocado with lemon juice, salt and pepper. Mix well. Dab buns with *Herb butter and toast in oven or grill. Spread tuna and avocado on buns and top with alfalfa sprouts or lettuce.

*Herb butter: 1 stick butter, garlic salt, basil, and rosemary. Mix together and melt butter over low heat.

New England Patriots
81 Tight End

RUSS FRANCIS

KAHUNA'S TUNA SANDWICH

After playing a game, even the most infinitesimal task is a real effort, but this is almost as easy as ordering a pizza.

FILLING:
1 can tuna, drained
3 hard boiled eggs, chopped
3 green onions, chopped (3 T.)
3 T. sweet pickle relish
salt
mayonnaise

cheddar cheese
tomato slices
Syrian pocket bread

Combine ingredients for filling. Cut Syrian loaves in half width-wise and add filling, tomato slices and cheese. Heat on a cookie sheet in 350° oven approximately 15—20 minutes. Ideally the cheese should be just on the verge of oozing forth. To catch it at this moment is to catch it at its peak. It also saves having to scrub burnt cheese off the cookie sheet. Makes 6 sandwiches.

*   *   *

Cleveland Browns
56 Linebacker

ROBERT LEE JACKSON

TUNA NOODLE CASSEROLE

8 oz. noodles cooked
2 cans (7 oz. each) tuna, well drained
1½ cups sour cream
¾ cup milk
1 can sliced mushrooms
1½ teas. salt
¼ teas. pepper
¼ cup grated parmesan cheese
2 T. butter or margarine, melted
top with ¼ cup bread crumbs

Bake at 350° until bubbly.

FLOYD PETERS

Detroit Lions
Defensive Line Coach

TURKEY CASSEROLE

This turkey casserole is great for informal company.

Use large deep casserole. Spread bottom with 1 large can tamales, sliced. Next layer, 2—4 oz. can mushrooms. Next pour over 8 oz. can tomato sauce. Next layer 1 rolled turkey roast (or chicken), diced. Then add ½ cup instant rice. Next layer 2 bunches chopped green onions. Pour over another 8 oz. can tomato sauce. Poke holes in casserole and pour 3 cans cream of chicken soup over top. Bake 325° for 1 hour 15 minutes. Grate ½ lb. sharp cheese on top. Serves 8—10.

* * *

HARRY HULMES

New Orleans Saints
Vice-President Player Personnel

BABY VEAL

1 lb. baby veal (sliced very thin)
¼ lb. butter
lemon juice, 1 T.
2 or 3 cloves of garlic
mozzarella cheese

Melt butter in 13½x8¾ pyrex dish. Put lemon juice and garlic in butter. Lay veal in butter. Bake in oven 350° for 20 minutes. Then cover meat with mozzarella cheese and return to oven until cheese melts. (You can cover meat with parmesan cheese also in the very beginning.)

Hall of Fame
Baltimore Colts
70 Tackle

ART DONOVAN

PAUPIETTES DE VIEU RICHELIEU

6 thinly sliced veal scallops	butter
1/2 lb. sausage meat	oil
pinch of all spice	1 lg. onion, chopped fine
1 shallot, chopped fine	2 cloves garlic, minced
1 egg	2 cups chicken stock
1/2 wine glass dry white wine	1 teas. tomato paste
chopped parsley	bouquet garni
swallow of cognac	3 tomatoes
salt and pepper	parsley

Pound the veal on a wet board with a wet meat hammer. Mix the sausage with allspice, minced shallot, egg, white wine, parsley, cognac, salt and pepper together. Spread this evenly over the scallops and roll them up. Tie with string as you would a parcel. Roll in flour and before cooking roll again in flour. Melt some butter and oil in a saute pan when hot put in veal birds to color them, which should take about 10 minutes. Keep turning slowly to brown on all sides. When veal has browned, remove it from the pan and pour out fat. Bake in oven at 375° for 45 minutes or until done. Serves 6.

•   •   •

Houston Oilers
16 Kicker

TONI FRITSCH

ORIGINAL WIENER SCHNITZEL

Pound veal very thin. Sprinkle with salt and pepper. Dip in egg, beaten slightly. Let stand 20 minutes. Dip in seasoned flour and crumbs. Saute slowly in a mixture of half olive oil and half butter until brown, 10 minutes. Serve with a green salad and parsley potatoes.

P.A.S.S.
the
Vegetables

CHUCK WEBER

Baltimore Colts
Assistant Coach—Defense

ASPARAGUS CASSEROLE

2 pkgs. frozen (or fresh) asparagus
1/2 can cream of mushroom soup
1/2 pt. sour cream
1/2 pkg. dry onion soup mix
1 can chop suey noodles

Cut asparagus in bite size pieces. Cook 10 minutes. Mix soup, sour cream and dry soup mix. Pour over asparagus. Bake at 350° for 1/2 hour. Add noodles last 10 minutes. Do not cover.

•   •   •

DAN SEKANOVICH

New York Jets
Assistant Coach

BAKED LIMA BEANS

Soak 1 box lima beans overnight. Boil until 1/2 done. Cut 1/2 lb. bacon in pieces. Cut 1/4 cup celery and onions. Fry in butter. Pour off juice from lima beans and save some juice. 2 cups can tomatoes. Put in casserole dish: 1 layer lima beans, then bacon, celery and onions (alternate). Then season. Add to juice, brown sugar and mustard to taste, a few dashes of ketchup and butter on top. Bake in 350° oven for 30—40 minutes.

•   •   •

MICKEY C. SHULER

New York Jets
82 Tight End

YELLOW WAX BEAN CASSEROLE

1 can yellow wax beans
1 can mushroom soup
1/2 chopped onion

1/2 cup grated cheese
bread crumbs

Mix all ingredients together in a casserole dish. Top with bread crumbs. Bake at 350° for 45 minutes.

Atlanta Falcons
32 Free Safety

RAY ESTERLING

BARBECUED BEANS

Great with grilled hamburgers.

1 onion diced
3 T. butter or margarine
2 one lb. cans pork 'n beans
2 cups catsup
2 T. brown sugar
1 T. honey
salt and pepper
3 strips bacon

Cook onion in butter until tender. Mix with pork and beans, catsup, brown sugar and honey in mixing bowl. Salt and pepper to taste. Lay strips of bacon in bottom of medium baking dish. Pour bean mixture into dish. Cover and bake at 350° until bubbly.

*   *   *

Detroit Lions
62 Guard

LYNN BODEN

BEAN CASSEROLE

This is a weight watcher recipe. . .

1½ cup cooked green beans
½ cup fresh mushrooms, sliced
2 oz. grated cheese
1 slice bread crumbs
¼ cup tomato juice
½ teas. mixed dried herbs (parsley, chives, basil, etc.)
salt and pepper

In a small casserole pan, layer vegetables, mushrooms, cheese and herbs. Sprinkle with salt and pepper. Stir in tomato juice and top with bread crumbs. Bake at 350° till hot and bubbly. Serves 2.

ALDEN ROCHE

Seattle
75 Defensive End

RED BEANS

On my return home after every football season, my dad always has my favorite meals waiting for me — Gumbo and Red Beans. I think about Gumbo and Red Beans, New Orleans style, all season long.

1 lb. red beans (dry)   pinch of sugar
1 medium onion   1 lb. pickled pork
1 clove garlic   1 teas. parsley
salt and pepper to taste

Place beans, garlic, pepper, salt, parsley and sugar in 5 qt. pot; cook until beans are tender (about 1 hour). Fry pickled pork and onions together in separate frying pan and add to beans; cook until meat is tender over slow heat about another hour. Serve over hot rice.

* * *

MICHAEL SIANI

Baltimore Colts
45 Wide Receiver

BROCCOLI WITH PASTA

1 head broccoli, cut into stalks   2 T. butter
1/2 lb. vermicelli pasta   1/2 cup plus 1 T. parmesan cheese
2 oz. olive oil   salt and pepper to taste
4—5 whole clove garlic   dried parsley

Bring 6 qts. water to boil. Add broccoli. Bring water to second boil and let broccoli cook 5 minutes. Add pasta and cook until tender. Remove from stove and drain most of water from pot. Add sauce.

Sauce: Brown whole garlic in oil. Add spices to taste and one T. grated cheese. Mix sauce with broccoli and pasta; just before serving sprinkle 1/2 cup cheese over top with butter.

Houston Oilers
29 Safety and Wide Receiver   **GUIDO ALBERT MERKENS, JR.**

BROCCOLI & RICE CASSEROLE

Cook 1 package of frozen broccoli, drain, set aside. Cook 1 cup of rice, drain, set aside. Saute ¼ cup of chopped celery and ¼ cup chopped onion in 2 T. butter until soft. Take a large casserole—mix together broccoli, rice, sauted vegetables, 1 can of cream of mushroom soup, and ½ cup shredded cheese. Top with another ½ cup of cheese, heat until warm and cheese is melted.

•   •   •

Dallas Cowboys
Assistant Coach   **MIKE DITKA**

GOLUMKI
Stuffed Cabbage
(Polish)

1½ cup rice	½ lb. ground beef
1 lg. head cabbage	1 teas. each salt and pepper
2 med. onion, chopped	1 small can sauerkraut
8 strips bacon	8 oz. can tomato sauce
pinch paprika	1 can tomato soup
½ lb. ground pork	1 T. sugar

Cook rice and let cool. Parboil cabbage and separate leaves using the largest. Cut ribs off and let cool. Saute onions with 5 strips of minced bacon and a pinch of paprika. Mix onions and bacon with ground meats. Thoroughly mix in cooked rice, salt and pepper. Roll cabbage with 1 heaping tablespoon of mixture in center. Thoroughly drain sauerkraut and spread on the bottom of small roaster. Take remains of cabbage head and dice and lay on top of sauerkraut. Place cabbage rolls tightly together on top of diced cabbage with seam side down. Pour cans of tomato sauce and soup over, and enough water to cover. Lay remaining strips of bacon on top. Sprinkle 1 T. sugar over rolls and simmer covered in 300° oven for 1½ hours. Uncover and simmer 30 minutes. Cooking time should not exceed 2 hours. Add more water if needed.

TERRY SCHMIDT

Chicago Bears
44 Defensive Back

CAULIFLOWER RECIPE

This is an excellent "Pot Luck" vegetable dish or for company. If you live where shrimp is not $6.95 lb. You can use shrimp instead of ham. (We originally received this recipe from a friend in Louisiana, when Terry played for the New Orleans Saints — where shrimp was plentiful!) Debbie.

1 lg. fresh cauliflower (cut up)	¼ cup of Chablis wine
1½ sticks of margarine	2 hard boiled eggs (chopped)
½ cup of flour	1 teas. garlic powder
2½ cups of milk	grated cheddar cheese
1½ bunches of green onions (chopped)	parmesan cheese
2 slices boiled ham (chopped)	bread crumbs

Boil cauliflower; melt margarine and combine flour, onions, ham, milk, and simmer for 15 minutes. Add hard boiled eggs, wine and garlic powder. Place cauliflower in 13x9 baking dish, and pour mixture over cauliflower. Sprinkle cheese and bread crumbs on top and bake for 25 minutes at 375°.

•   •   •

TOM PRATT

New Orleans Saints
Defensive Line Coach

BAR-B-Q CORN

6 ears sweet corn
salt water
butter

Loosen husks and remove corn silk, then replace husks and tie with string. Soak in salt water for 4 hours. Remove corn from salt water and place on Bar-B-Q grill for 1 hour, turning every 20 minutes. After 1 hour, pull husks and dip in melted butter or turn corn on solid pound of butter. Salt to taste. Serves 6.

Los Angeles Rams
39 Running Back

ROD PHILLIPS

CORN CASSEROLE

A delicious meal in one dish.

1 lb. ground beef	*1 cup sour cream*
1 can whole corn	*1 pkg. of elbow macaroni*
1 can cream of mushroom soup	*1 onion*
1 can cream of chicken soup	*1 bell pepper*
1 can pimento	*½ cup celery*

Prepare macaroni as directed on package; drain and add all ingredients. Mix well and bake 30—40 minutes at 350⁰. May be frozen for later use.

• • •

Chicago Bears
General Manager

JIM FINKS

DOWN SOUTH OKRA

If you don't like okra, you'll like this—if you like okra, you'll love this!

6 oz. pkg. frozen cut okra
16 oz. canned stewed tomatoes
6 slices bacon fried crisp and chopped
  (reserve 3 T. bacon grease)
½ cup chopped onion
1 T. vinegar

Bring okra to boil in ½ cup water and 1 T. vinegar. Simmer about 3 minutes until okra separates. Thoroughly drain (vinegar will remove, what do I call it—that slippery juice—from okra). Cook onion in hot skillet in 3 T. bacon grease on one side of skillet. Brown okra on other side of skillet. Cook both until okra is slightly brown and onion is soft (3—4 minutes). Add tomatoes and bacon. Simmer about 8 minutes, stirring occasionally and gently (so as not to break okra). Serve with corn bread and salad and chicken or fish.

THOMAS LYNCH

Seattle Seahawks
61 Left Guard

PEPPERS — ONIONS — SQUASH

Colorful and attractive. P.A.S.S.

1/4 cup oil or butter	1/2 teas. sugar
2 lg. green peppers	1/4 teas. oregano
1 lg. onion	1/4 teas. basil
2 lg. yellow summer squash	dash salt and pepper
1 lg. tomato, cut up	1 teas. vinegar

Heat oil in frying pan, cook cut up vegetables to desired doneness. Add remaining ingredients and simmer for approximately 15 minutes. Depending on size of party, amount of vegetable varies.

•   •   •

JOE DEVLIN

Buffalo Bills
70 Tackle

BEER BATTER FOR ONION RINGS

3/4 cup flour	1 teas. oil
1/2 cup flat beer at room temp.	1 egg, separated
salt to taste	

Place the flour in a bowl and stir in the beer, salt and oil. Stir to blend. There should be a few small lumps. Cover the bowl with plastic wrap and let stand in a warm place about three hours. Stir in the egg yolk. When ready to cook, beat the white until stiff and fold in. Dip onion rings into batter and deep fry.

Pittsburgh Steelers
Assistant Coach

DICK HOAK

SHREDDED POTATO CASSEROLE

8 potatoes
1 teas. dry mustard
1½ teas. salt
½ cup shredded sharp cheese
½ pt. sour cream
1 cup milk

Boil potatoes with skin till firm. Peel and shred into buttered casserole. In sauce pan add remaining ingredients. Heat until cheese melts. Pour over potatoes. Do not stir. Sprinkle with paprika and dot with butter. Cover and refrigerate for 24 hours. Remove from refrigerator for one hour before baking. Bake at 350° for one hour uncovered. (May be frozen.)

•   •   •

Dallas Cowboys
63 Defensive Tackle

LARRY COLE

LEFSA
(Norwegian Delicacy)

8 cups mashed potatoes
½ cup whipping cream, not whipped
8 heaping T. butter or oleo
1 T. salt
4 cups flour-scant

Peel potatoes, cook, then mash with butter, cream and salt. Let them get cold. Mix in flour and roll out rounds of dough paper thin (using a grooved, Norwegian lefsa rolling pin) on lightly floured board. Bake rounds of lefsa on pancake griddle. Serve with butter and sugar rollups.

GEORGE PERLES

Pittsburgh Steelers
Assistant Head Coach

LITHUANIAN KUGALE

Serves a crowd. It's really excellent and my specialty.

> 8 lbs. Idaho potatoes peeled & HAND grated
>   (Do NOT use blender!)
> 6 eggs—slightly beaten
> 1/2 lb. melted butter
> 1 lg. onion grated
> 1 teas. salt

Combine ingredients. Pour into greased roaster and bake 2 hours at 375° (until brown on top and set in center). Slice and serve with butter and sour cream. To serve left overs, fry in butter and serve with sour cream.

•   •   •

PETE ROZELLE

N.F.L.
Commissioner

POTATOE PANCAKES

> 4—6 potatoes (2 cups grated)
> 1/2 onion grated
> 1 teas. salt
> 1/4 teas. pepper
>
> 2 eggs
> 1 T. flour
> 2 T. chopped parsley (opt.)
> 1/4 teas. nutmeg (opt.)

Mix all ingredients. Heat frying pan (I use my iron one for this) with shortening. It is nice to add a little bacon grease for flavor. Drop large spoonfuls of potato mixture into the pan and brown the pancakes over medium heat. Turn to brown on the other side. Drain well on paper towels.

TO MAKE AHEAD: Reheat the pancakes on a large cookie sheet at 375° until very hot.

TO FREEZE: Freeze in container (foil pie pans are ideal) between layers of saran. Defrost then reheat as above.

MICHAEL J. FRANCKOWIAK
PARTY POTATOES

2 lb. hash brown potatoes (frozen)	1/2 cup chopped onions
1/2 cup of melted butter	1 can cream of chicken soup
1 teas. salt	1 carton sour cream (12 oz.)
1/4 teas. pepper	

Defrost the potatoes, mix in ingredients and put in a 13x9 inch baking dish. Top the potatoes with 2 cups of crushed corn flakes mixed with 1/4 cup melted butter. Bake at 350° for 45 minutes. Serves 12. Let it cool a few minutes before serving.

* * *

JOE CAMPBELL

PIEROGI (DOUGH)

5 cups flour	6 egg yolks
1/4 lb. butter	3 eggs
1 cup sour cream	pinch salt
3/4 cup water	

Make a mound out of the flour, then make a well in the center. Place egg yolks and eggs in the center, cutting in the flour with a knife and adding water and salt. Knead until firm. Cut in three parts. Roll dough out thinly, then cut circles with a cup. Place a small amount of filling off center on each circle of dough. Fold over and seal by moistening edge with water and putting pressure on edges for a firm seal. Boil a pot of water. Add salt. Drop Pierogi into boiling water. Cook lightly for 5 minutes using a low flame. Remove gently with strainer spoon and brown in butter or margarine in frying pan. Serve with sour cream.

PIEROGI (FILLING)

1 cup cottage cheese (dry)	1 T. onions (chopped fine)
1 cup whipped potatoes	salt, pepper to taste

Combine ingredients and mix lightly. Let cool and fill circles with desired amount.

DON TESTERMAN

Seattle Seahawks
Running Back

SCALLOP POTATOES

6—8 potatoes, peeled and sliced very thin
1 lg. pkg. shredded cheddar cheese
1 can cream of celery soup
1 can cream of mushroom soup
1 large white onion chopped finely

Combine cream of celery and cream of mushroom soups in a bowl. In deep casserole dish put a layer of potatoes, sprinkle some onions, cover with soup mixture, and sprinkle on some cheese. Put another layer of potatoes, onions, soup and cheese. Continue to layer until casserole dish is full. Be sure to complete each layering process. Bake covered at 350° for approximately two hours, or until potatoes are tender. Remove cover the last 15 minutes.

•   •   •

RAY WERSCHING

San Francisco 49ers
14 Place Kicker

ARMENIAN PILAF

½ cup melted butter
2 cups of wide egg noodles
2 cups of converted rice
4 cups of chicken broth

Brown uncooked noodles in butter until it gets foamy. Add rice and pour in the broth. Bring to boil in covered skillet. Simmer on low for 35 minutes. Do not lift lid until last 10 minutes, stir at this point. Makes 6 to 8 servings.

Baltimore Colts
42 Defensive Back

LLOYD MUMPHORD

LOUISIANA DIRTY RICE

2½ cups rice, cooked firm　　　　*1 lg. onion, finely chopped*
½ cup oil　　　　　　　　　*½ cup finely chopped celery*
2 lbs. chicken liver, finely chopped　　*1 teas. cornstarch*
* (use a meat grinder or blender)*　　*2½ cups water*
3 sprigs parsley　　　　*3 cloves garlic, finely chopped*
1 T. soy sauce　　　*½ cup finely chopped bell pepper*

In large deep pot, saute chicken liver in oil until firm. Add onions and cook until soft. Add water, garlic, celery, bell pepper and salt and pepper to taste. Let simmer on low heat about 2 hours or until all ingredients are well done. Mix cornstarch, soy sauce, and a little water. Add to liver paste and let simmer about 15 minutes. There should be a thin gravy; if gravy has boiled out, add a little water and let simmer a few minutes more. Remove from heat and thoroughly mix hot cooked rice to liver sauce. Sprinkle chopped parsley over top, cover until ready to serve.

For freezing purposes. You can make a batch of liver and freeze. If only one person feels up to eating dirty rice, just defrost a little and put in skillet and warm, then add cooked rice, as much as you plan to eat.

*　　*　　*

Miami Dolphins
53 Linebacker

BOB MATHESON

BROWNED RICE

1 medium onion
1 stick margarine
1 cup rice

Brown the rice and add 2 cans consomme soup. Pour into a baking dish and cover. Bake at 300° for 2 hours. This goes with about anything and is simple to do. Serves 8.

MONTE CLARK

Detroit Lions
Head Coach

RICE PILAF

1 cup rice (Uncle Ben's or Long Grain)
1 stick margarine
1 cup vermicelli (broken up)
1½ cup chicken broth (canned)
1 cup water
1 teas. salt
dash pepper

Melt margarine in 2 qt. pan. Add vermicelli to margarine until browned, stirring constantly and breaking up. Add rice and remove from heat and mix thoroughly. Add broth and water. Bring to boil, then lower heat. Simmer for 20 minutes until water is absorbed and rice is soft. Turn heat off and let sit a few minutes. Stir once, then serve.

* * *

STEVE JONES

St. Louis Cardinals
34 Running Back

SQUASH LOAF

1 lb. squash
cracker crumbs (15 crackers)
1½ cups grated cheese
1 egg
salt and pepper to taste

Cook squash until tender and then mash up, adding egg, salt and pepper. Put one half in a well greased baking dish, then put a layer of grated cheese, sprinkle cracker crumbs on top. Make a second layer with remaining squash, cover with grated cheese and crackers. Bake in oven for 35—40 minutes at 375°.

New Orleans Saints
84 Wide Receiver

RICH MAUTI

SPINACH—RICOTTA ROLL UPS

2 lbs. ricotta
small pkg. mozzarella, grated
2 lb. grated cheese (your choice)
pinch of salt

1 box of chopped spinach—cooked
and drained very dry
1½ lb. lasagna or
manicotti noodles

Cook pasta with a tablespoon of oil and salt until al dente. Drain, put in cold water. Take one noodle at a time. One tablespoon of filling, spread and roll up. Put roll-ups in a pan with sauce on the bottom, just a small layer. Place them side by side. When placed, pour your sauce over all the roll-ups. Put grated cheese and grated mozzarella on top and bake at 350°, about 20—25 minutes until hot through.

SAUCE

2 cans of Italian tomatoes
(2 lb. cans)
(break up tomatoes in blender)
1 can of paste
2 cloves of garlic

small onion (opt.)
basil (to taste)
salt
grated pepper

Add sausages and meatballs. Cook slowly for about 3 hours until sauce coats spoon. Not too thick.

* * *

Miami Dolphins
President and Owner

JOE ROBBIE

BARLEY CASSEROLE

Melt ¼ cup butter. Stir in 2 medium chopped onions and ¾ lb. mushrooms, trimmed and sliced. Cook until golden and tender. Add 1 cup pearl barley and cook until barley is delicate brown. Transfer to casserole. Add 3 pimentoes and 2 cups chicken stock. Salt and pepper to taste. Bake at 350° for 1 hour and 15 minutes covered. If barley seems dry, add more stock. Then add 1 lb. almonds and bake 30 minutes longer uncovered.

LARRY CSONKA

Miami Dolphins
39 Fullback

CREAMED CELERY WITH ALMONDS

4 cups celery, sliced 1 in. thick
1/2 cup milk
1 T. finely chopped parsley or chives
1/2 cup toasted diced almonds
10 1/2 oz. can condensed cream of celery soup
1 teas. instant minced onion
1 T. pimento, chopped finely

Cook celery in boiling salted water in saucepan for 5 minutes. Blend soup, onion, parsley, pimento, and milk. Combine with celery (after draining). Pour into 1 1/2 qt. casserole. Sprinkle almonds on top. Bake at 350° for 20 minutes until hot and lightly browned. Serves 6.

*   *   *

JERRY GOLSTEYN

Baltimore Colts
12 Quarterback

VEGETABLE FRY

1 small cabbage
3 small zucchini
2 large tomatoes
3 medium onions

3 cloves garlic
freshly ground black pepper
1/2-1 T. curry powder
1/4 cup olive oil

Thinly slice cabbage. Chop zucchini and tomatoes. Slice onions in rounds and then in half. Put oil in frying pan. When it's hot put in garlic and onions, saute for about 2 minutes. Add squash and saute. Add coleslaw, saute until it wilts a bit. Add tomatoes, pepper and curry powder. Stir and saute for a few more minutes. Serves about 6.

Los Angeles Rams
89 Defensive End

FRED DRYER

DRYER'S DIET

You'll be surprised how fulfilled you will be after you sit down to this organic delicacy.

2 firm yellow onions, sliced evenly
2 heads broccoli tops
2 carrots sliced
1 handful cauliflower tops
1 complete stalk celery sliced
3 red rose potatoes sliced thinly
2 handfuls of beautiful bean sprouts
1 yellow crook neck squash sliced
1 zucchini sliced

(Place more dense vegetables close to the bottom of the steamer.) After veggies have steamed, remove, place in a bowl and lightly sprinkle with olive oil, and caraway seeds and garlic powder.

* * *

Miami Dolphins
49 Safety

CHARLIE BABB

ZUCCHINI CASSEROLE

1 lb. zucchini
1 onion
1 green pepper, diced
1 can of tomatoes chopped, no juice

1 teas. garlic salt
1 teas. salt
1 teas. accent
1 teas. pepper

Cut zucchini into rounds. Mix garlic salt, accent, and pepper. Sprinkle over layers. Make 2 layers topping each with grated cheddar cheese. Bake one hour with lid at 350°.

RUSS THOMAS

Detroit Lions
Vice President

RUSS' ZUCCHINI CASSEROLE

3 med. zucchini
1/2 green pepper
3 T. flour
1/2 teas. ground cloves
3 T. brown sugar

1 small onion
1 lg. can tomatoes
3 T. butter
1/2 teas. cinnamon

Melt butter, add flour and blend, add tomatoes and spices, sugar and salt and pepper to taste. Cook until lightly thickened. Cool. Slice zucchini, onion and green pepper in a 3 qt. casserole. Pour tomato mixture over vegetables and sprinkle generously with parmesan cheese. Bake 1 hour at 350°.

• • •

JEAN BARRETT

San Francisco 49ers
77 Offensive Tackle

FETTUCCINE AL BURRO

1/4 lb. soft butter
1/4 cup heavy cream
1/2 cup grated parmesan cheese
1 cup fettuccine or egg noodles

Cream the butter until it is light and fluffy. Beat in the cream a little at a time, and then, a few tablespoons at a time, beat in cheese. Heat casserole dish in 250° oven while cooking the fettuccine. (You may substitute egg noodles.) After the noodles are cooked, put them in the hot casserole dish. Then add the creamed mixture and toss with the noodles.

Philadelphia Eagles
7 Quarterback

RON JAWORSKI

LAZY MAN'S PEIROGI A LA RON JAWORSKI

8 oz. sauerkraut	*2 onions*
8 oz. elbow macaroni	*1 stick butter*
4 oz. mushrooms (drained)	

Boil noodles as directed. Saute onions and mushrooms in butter until soft. Add the sauerkraut to this mixture and mix together thoroughly. Cook 8—10 minutes until heated through. Mix with macaroni and enjoy. Serves 6—8 people.

•   •   •

Alumni
Miami Dolphins
85 Linebacker

NICK BUONICONTI

MACARONI PIE

Great recipe to prepare ahead and eat at room temperature with salad and French bread.

2 cups elbow macaroni	*¼ cup parsley*
1 dozen eggs	*salt and pepper to taste*
½ cup grated romano cheese	

Parboil macaroni and drain. Combine remaining ingredients and stir in macaroni. Preheat oiled fry pan, and pour in ingredients, cover and cook on low for 10 minutes. Loosen sides and turn over into another preheated oiled fry pan, cook again for 10 minutes. The macaroni pie is easy to remove from fry pan, and may be served at any desired temperature (hot or cold).

GUS CIFELLI

Alumni
Detroit Lions
71 Tackle

MANICOTTI

SHELLS:

6 eggs
1 cup flour
1 cup milk

Mix with beater and pour small amount, enough to cover bottom of pan, into 6 inch cast iron fry pan. When edges curl, less than a minute over medium to low heat, adjust heat so they don't burn, remove from pan.

Makes approximately 27—28 crepe shells.

FILLING

1 egg
1 lb. ricotta cheese (more if necessary—don't make too loose)
salt and pepper (to taste)
grated imported romano cheese (sprinkle small amount in filling)

Mix ingredients. Stuff crepe shells with filling. Top filling with grated (larger grate) mozarella cheese, wrap. Line baking dish with thin layer of spaghetti sauce and sprinkle finely grated romano cheese over sauce. Fill pan with manicotti crepes, cover with more sauce and grated romano cheese. Cover pan with aluminum foil and bake 45 minutes to 1 hour at 325°. If frozen, defrost before baking.

JOHN PETERCUSKIE

MILLION DOLLAR SPAGHETTI

7 oz. pkg. thin spaghetti
1 T. butter
1½ lbs. ground beef
salt and pepper
½ lb. Italian sausage
1 T. minced green pepper

2—8 oz. cans tomato sauce
8 oz. cream cheese
¼ cup sour cream
½ lb. cottage cheese
⅓ cup cut up scallions
2 T. melted butter

Cook spaghetti and drain. Saute beef in butter until brown. Add tomato sauce, salt and pepper. Remove from heat. Combine cottage cheese, cream cheese, sour cream, scallions, and green pepper. In a square 2 qt. casserole spread one half the spaghetti and cover with cheese mixture, and fried sausage. Add remainder of spaghetti and pour butter over spaghetti. Spread tomato meat sauce over top. Chill. Remove from refrigerator 20 minutes before baking. Bake at 350° for 45 minutes or until hot and bubbly. Serve with green salad and garlic bread.

P.A.S.S.
the
Eggs and Cheese

LYNN CHANDNOIS

Alumni
Pittsburgh Steelers
49 Halfback

BACON & EGG CASSEROLE

2 or 3 lg. onions, sliced thin
1 can cheddar cheese soup
¼ cup butter or margarine
8 hard cooked eggs sliced
½ cup milk
1 cup shredded cheddar cheese
1 lb. bacon cooked and crumbled

Cook onions in margarine until tender (not brown). Place in shallow 1½ qt. baking dish. Combine cheese soup and milk in saucepan, add cheddar cheese and stir, until cheese melts. Place eggs on top of onions. Pour on sauce. Sprinkle with bacon. Bake at 350° for about 20 minutes. Serve on toast. Can be made ahead of time and kept in refrigerator. Also can be frozen. Serves 4.

* * *

BARRY DARROW

New Orleans Saints
63 Offensive Right Tackle

MOM'S SPECIAL BREAKFAST

This is a recipe my mom made up which has become a family favorite.

Beat 6 eggs, add 2 T. flour, 3 T. milk, 1 T. sugar. Mix all ingredients either in blender or with hand mixer. Melt 2 T. butter in electric frypan set at 350°. Coat bottom of pan with butter. Pour ½ batter in frypan and tip pan till mixture coats bottom of pan evenly. When mixture is set, put lid on pan for about 3—4 minutes. Flip over and cook other side for about a minute. Remove from pan, put on plate. Spread with butter and fresh sliced strawberries in season or with freezer strawberry jam. Roll and eat. 2 servings.

Buffalo Bills
Head Coach

CHUCK KNOX

MUSHROOM FRITTATA

Very good with tossed salad, garlic bread for a luncheon.

1 cup sliced fresh mushrooms   *⅓ cup chopped onion*
⅓ cup chopped green pepper   *1 cup chopped zucchini*
1 teas. minced garlic   *⅓ cup Half & Half*
2 T. cooking oil   *5 eggs*
½ teas. salt   *¼ teas. pepper*
1½ cups soft bread cubes,   1 cup cheddar cheese—shredded
*   lightly packed*
8 oz. cream cheese, cut into ½ inch cubes
*   (place in freezer a few minutes to make*
*   hard for cutting)*

Saute: mushrooms, onion, green pepper, zucchini and garlic in oil until crisp—tender. Beat eggs with cream, salt and pepper. Add cream cheese cubes, stirring lightly to coat with egg so they stay intact. Combine mushroom mixture, bread cubes and cheddar cheese. Toss lightly. Add egg, cream cheese mixture to this. Stir thoroughly, but lightly, so cream cheese cubes are intact, but mixture is distributed evenly. Pour into a well greased 9-inch pie plate (glass). Bake in a preheated oven 350°, 45 minutes, or until set in center and browned. Cool 5—10 minutes before cutting into wedges. Serves 4—6.

•   •   •

St. Louis Cardinals
17 Quarterback

JIM HART

JALAPENO PEPPER PIE

Grease pyrex pie pan with butter. Line with chopped jalapeno peppers (remove seeds). Add ½ lb. grated sharp cheddar cheese. Beat 4 eggs until foamy; pour over cheese. Bake at 275° for 45 minutes or microwave on high, 8 minutes, turning pan ½ revolution after 4 minutes. Let it sit a few minutes to firm up the middle.

TOM BROOKSHIER

Alumni
Philadelphia Eagles
40 Right Defensive Cornerback
CBS Announcer

CHILE AND MUSHROOM OMELETS

Tom is from New Mexico and loves hot Mexican food! Barbara.

¼ cup chopped green chilies
4 medium sized mushrooms, sliced
1 small onion, sliced thin
½ lb. Canadian bacon, chopped into small pieces
½ lb. sharp cheddar cheese, grated

FILLING: Melt butter in medium sized pan. Add all ingredients except cheese and saute until onions are limp and mushrooms tender.

OMELETS: For each omelet, you will need 2 eggs, 1 T. cream, 1 T. butter, and dash salt. Mix eggs, cream and salt well, preferably with a wire whisk. Melt butter in omelet pan (or 7-8 inch skillet with sloping sides) until golden brown. Add eggs, scrambling just enough so that all the egg sets cooked. When omelet is shiny and just moist on top, remove from heat and spoon on ½ cup filling and top with 1 T. grated cheese. Fold omelet in half and flip onto serving plate. Prepare additional omelets in same way.

• • •

RON McDOLE

Buffalo Bills
Washington Redskins
79 Defensive End

McDOLE'S NON-PLAYING SUNDAY EGGS

dash worcestershire
dash garlic salt
grated cheese, both mild & sharp
mushrooms, fresh 1 lb. or more
pieces of crumbled sausage, bacon and/or ham (opt.)

¼ lb. butter
eggs, according to number of people

Saute mushrooms in butter in pan. Then melt cheese and add other ingredients. Whip eggs in blender. Fold in pan. Cook til set. Use freshly grated pepper.

Miami Dolphins
58 Outside Linebacker

KIM BOKAMPER

FRUIT AND CHEESE OMELET

1 teas. cornstarch
2 teas. honey
3 T. orange juice
1 teas. lemon juice
¼ cup shredded Swiss or cheddar cheese

¾ cup mixture fresh fruit
(such as sliced strawberries,
bananas, blueberries, etc.)
1 recipe omelet (plain)

In small saucepan combine cornstarch and honey; stir in orange juice and lemon juice. Cook and stir till mixture is thickened and bubbly. Stir in fruit to heat through, keep warm. Prepare plain omelet. Use some fruit mixture to fill omelet. Fold omelet. Top with remaining fruit and cheese. To melt, place in oven for 3—5 minutes.

• • •

Atlanta Falcons
45 Safety

TOM MORIARTY

ITALIAN OMELETTE

4 eggs
⅓ cup grated romano cheese
1 clove garlic, finely chopped
1 pinch parsley
salt and pepper to taste

Mix all the ingredients together. Beat well with a fork. Fry in hot oil. May be eaten as a sandwich in bread or just plain.

PAT LEAHY

New York Jets
5 Placekicker

REUBEN OMELET

My own specialty.

3 eggs
½ cup of cooked sauerkraut, sauteed in butter and onions
2 slices of cooked corned beef, chopped finely
grated swiss cheese
pinch of chili powder

Beat 3 eggs and pour into a heated 8-inch skillet to make an omelet. Just before folding the omelet, add the sauerkraut, corned beef, cheese, and chili powder.

•   •   •

RICK MOSER

Pittsburgh Steelers
39 Running Back

ARTICHOKE QUICHE

1 pkg. frozen artichoke hearts, cooked
8 oz. mozzarella cheese, grated
½ cup cream
4 eggs, well mixed
¼ cup parmesan cheese, grated
1 frozen deep dish pie shell

Saute artichokes in a little olive oil (or margarine) and clove garlic for 5 minutes. Let cool. Remove garlic and mash artichokes well (or cut up in small pieces). Mix mozzarella, eggs and grated cheese. Add artichokes. Pour into frozen uncooked, deep dish pie shell. Bake 350° for 45—60 minutes until brown.

Pittsburgh Steelers
74 Offensive Tackle

RAY PINNEY

BROCCOLI QUICHE

pastry for single 9" pie
2 cups chopped fresh broccoli
1/4 cup sliced scallions
2/3 cup chicken broth
1/2 teas. salt

1/4 cup grated parmesan,
divided in half
1 cup shredded Swiss cheese
3 eggs
1/2 cup whipping cream
1/8 t. tabasco

Line a 10-inch quiche dish with pastry. Prick with fork. Bake at 450° for 5 minutes. Remove from oven. Sprinkle crust with 2 T. parmesan. Layer half broccoli, then half the Swiss cheese, then 1/2 the scallions. Repeat layers with other half of the ingredients. Beat eggs. To eggs mixture, add broth, cream salt and tabasco. Mix well. Pour over broccoli. Sprinkle top with 2 T. parmesan. Bake at 450° for 10 minutes. Lower heat to 325° and bake for 20 minutes longer. Let stand 10 minutes and serve.

* * *

San Diego Chargers
52 Linebacker

RAYMOND PRESTON, JR.

QUICHE LORRAINE

Ideal luncheon dish served with tossed salad.

9-inch CRUST, unbaked
1 cup unsifted flour
1 teas. salt
1/3 cup butter or margarine
3 or 4 T. ice water

FILLING:
1 onion
1 T. butter
6 slices crisp crumbled bacon
1/4 lb. Swiss cheese, diced
4 beaten eggs, slightly
2 cups light cream
1/8 teas. white pepper
1/8 teas. ground nutmeg

Saute 1 onion in 1 T. butter until tender and cool. Line unbaked crust with crumbled bacon and diced cheese. Combine remaining ingredients with onion. Pour into crust. Bake at 375° for about 35 minutes. Test for doneness—serve hot. Serves 6.

MARK MARKOVICH

Detroit Lions
68 Center

QUICHE MUSHROOMS

It's difficult to eat only a few of these!

2 lbs. lg. mushrooms
6 strips bacon
6 T. butter
2 T. minced green onions

2 eggs
½ cup heavy cream
2½ cups grated swiss cheese
½ teas. salt

Remove mushroom stems and chop stems finely. Saute bacon til crisp and crumbly. Pour fat from skillet. Using same skillet, melt butter. Add mushroom caps and brush with butter. Remove caps to large baking dish. Add onions and stems to butter and saute 3 minutes. In separate bowl, beat eggs, add cream, cheese, salt, bacon and mushroom mixture. Fill caps. Bake at 350º for 25—30 minutes. Serves 6—8.

•   •   •

MARK ALAN MULLANEY

Minnesota Vikings
77 Defensive End

WILLY'S SPECIAL

1 lb. hamburger
1 pkg. of frozen spinach
minced onions
soy sauce
6 eggs, scrambled

Fry hamburger in small pieces until brown adding minced onions and soy sauce to taste. Add cooked frozen spinach and mix. Scramble 6 eggs lightly. When serving, put eggs on top of mixture. Serve with soy sauce. 4 servings.

Baltimore Colts
11 Quarterback

GREG LANDRY

QUARTERBACK QUICHE

PASTRY:

1 cup plus 2 T. flour　　　　　　　　　　*3 T. shortening*
dash salt　　　　　　　　　　　　　　*2 to 5 T. ice cold milk*
3 T. firm butter

Put flour and salt in bowl. Using fingers, cut butter and shortening into flour. Work quickly and lightly. Rub flour and fat through fingertips until mixture is fine and mealy. Mix the dough gently as you add cold milk, 1 T. at a time. Add milk until mixture just gathers into a firm yet crumbly ball. Do not force the dough together. The less milk the flakier the pastry will be. Roll between 2 pieces of waxed paper. Line pan. Prick dough with fork.

CUSTARD

1 cup whipping cream　　　　　　　　*4 egg yolks*
pinch of salt, cayenne, nutmeg

Blend above together. Fill shell with ½ lb. Grugue or Swiss cheese or both. Add 1 cup crisp bacon and 1 to 2 T. onion. Pour custard over cheese, bacon and onions. Bake at 375° for 35—45 minutes or until custard is puffed and pastry is nicely browned. Allow to rest 5 minutes before serving.

• • •

Green Bay Packers
81 Tight End

RICH McGEORGE

EGG — CHEESE SOUFFLE

9½x13 buttered baking dish　　　　　*½ teas. dry mustard*
cubes or strips of buttered　　　　　*1 teas. brown sugar*
　bread to line bottom of pan　*½ teas. worcestershire sauce*
6 beaten eggs　　　　　　　　　　*½ teas. paprika*
3 cups milk, cream or Half & Half　*1½ cups grated cheese*

Pour egg mixture over bread and refrigerate overnight. Set baking dish in dish of water to bake for one hour at 300°.

LAMAR HUNT

Hall of Fame
Kansas City Chiefs
Owner

DELUXE SHRIMP SOUFFLE

8 slices slightly dry bread,
trimmed, buttered, cubed
2 cups cooked shrimp
1—3 oz. can broiled sliced
mushrooms, drained
1/2 lb. mild cheese, grated

3 eggs
1/2 teas. salt
1/2 teas. dry mustard
dash pepper
dash paprika
2 cups heavy cream

Place half of bread crumbs in a greased seven by eleven inch baking dish. Add shrimp, mushrooms and half the cheese. Top with remaining bread and cheese. Beat together eggs and seasonings. Add milk and pour over all. Bake at 325° for 45—50 minutes. Best made and refrigerated overnight before cooking. Serves eight.

•   •   •

ROGER STAUBACH

Dallas Cowboys
12 Quarterback

HOT CRAB SOUFFLE

8 slices bread
2 cups crab or shrimp
1/2 cup mayonnaise
1 onion, chopped
1 green pepper, chopped

1 cup celery chopped
3 cups milk
4 eggs
1 can mushroom soup
grated cheese

Dice half of bread into baking dish. Mix crab or shrimp, mayonnaise, onion, green pepper, celery and spread over diced bread. Trim crusts from remaining four slices and place trimmed slices over shrimp or crab mixture. Mix eggs and milk together and pour over mixture. Place in refrigerator overnight. Bake in 325° oven for 15 minutes. Take from oven and pour soup over the top. Top with cheese and paprika. Bake one hour in 325° oven. Serves 12.

Denver Broncos
41 Halfback

ROB LYTLE

CHEESE STRATA
Brunch

2 cups (3 slices) bread cubes,
  crusts trimmed
½ lb. sharp cheddar cheese, cubed
½ lb. bacon, cooked & crumbled
  (ham or shrimp may be substituted)
¼ cup butter, melted

½ lb. mushrooms
3 large eggs
2 cups milk
1 teas. prepared mustard
¼ teas. salt

Place half the bread cubes in a 1½ qt. casserole. Layer half the cheese, bacon and butter. Repeat layers and arrange mushrooms on top. Beat eggs, milk, mustard and salt and pour over the layered mixture. Set casserole in pan of hot water. Bake uncovered at 300° for 1½ hours. 6 servings. This is better if prepared in advance and refrigerated overnight until baking time.

* * *

Baltimore Colts
Head Coach

MIKE McCORMACK

FAMILY FONDUE

1 pkg. onion soup mix
1 lb. sharp cheddar cheese, grated

2 cups tomato juice
2 teas. lemon juice

Blend juices and soup mix. Heat in double boiler. Add cheese gradually after the mixture is hot. Put in fondue pot or chafing dish after all the cheese is melted. Add tomato juice to thin as needed or to taste. Serve with chunks of French, Italian, pumpernickel, or rye bread. Great after the game!

DOUG PLANK

Chicago Bears
46 Free Safety

QUICK CHEESE FONDUE

1 can (10¾ oz.) condensed cheddar cheese soup, undiluted
1 cup commercial French onion dip
1 cup shredded sharp cheddar cheese
½ teas. dry mustard
2 dashes cayenne (red) pepper

Combine all the ingredients and heat over medium, stirring occasionally.
Serve with cubes of French bread, mushrooms, and cauliflower.

P.A.S.S.
the
Bread

Hall of Fame
Chicago Bears
Owner

GEORGE S. HALAS

BANANA BREAD

⅔ cup shortening
⅔ cup sugar
2 well beaten eggs
1 cup mashed ripe bananas
1¾ cup sifted flour

¾ teas. soda
1¼ teas. cream of tartar
½ teas. salt
½ cup bran (breakfast cereal)
½ cup chopped nuts (opt.)

Cream shortening and sugar, add eggs and bananas. Sift together dry ingredients and add to mixture. Finally add bran and mix well. Bake in a 4½x13 pan or 2 small ones. Bake for one hour until done. Bake at 350°.

* * *

Buffalo Bills
Defensive Backfield Coach

JIM WAGSTAFF

BASIC WHITE BREAD

1 cup warm water (not hot—110°-115°)
¼ cup dry yeast
1 T. sugar
3½ cups lukewarm milk (canned) or potato water,
    or ½ water and milk
6 T. honey
4 teas. salt
¼ cup oil
14 cups flour

Measure into bowl: 1 cup warm water, yeast and sugar. Add, stirring to dissolve, remaining ingredients except flour. Stir in half of 14 cups of flour. Mix with spoon until smooth. Add remaining flour until dough can be handled easily. Knead dough until smooth and elastic, and no longer sticky. Cover and let rise in warm place until dough shows ripe test (press 2 fingers into dough. If it leaves indentation then dough is ready.) Punch down and let rise again (about 30 minutes). Divide dough into 4 equal portions. Shape into loaves. Let rise and bake at 400° for 10 minutes, continue baking at 375° for 30 minutes. Brush top with butter upon removing from oven. Makes 4 loaves.

KENNETH HUFF

Baltimore Colts
62 Offensive Guard

DATE NUT BREAD

Great served warm with butter.

Put into bowl & pour water over:
1 cup chopped dates
1 cup boiling water
1 teas. baking soda
1 cup sugar

Sift together:
2 cups flour
1/2 teas. salt
1/2 teas. baking powder

To first mixture add 1 unbeaten egg, 2 T. melted butter, 1 teas. vanilla, 1/2 cup chopped pecans and flour mixture. Mix well. Put into loaf pan lined with waxed paper. Bake 1 hour at 325°.

* * *

GEORGE COLLINS

St. Louis Cardinals
66 Offensive Lineman

EGG BREAD

Sift together:2 cups corn meal
1/4 cup flour
1/2 teas. soda
1/4 teas. baking powder
1/2 teas. salt

1 egg
2 T. cooking oil
1 1/4 cups of milk

Break egg in mixing bowl and beat. Add milk and cooking oil and mix. Then sift in the meal and flour and mix making a soft batter even if you have to add a little more milk. Pour into greased 8 or 9 inch round pan and bake about 25 or 30 minutes in a preheated oven at 450°.

St. Louis Cardinals
57 Linebacker

SEAN CLANCY

EASY IRISH SODA BREAD

4 cups bisquick
2 T. sugar
½ cup raisins (or more if you like)

1 teas. caraway seeds (opt.)
1½ cups buttermilk
1½ teas. baking soda

Mix dry ingredients. Add baking soda to buttermilk and then add to dry mixture. Mix. Put in greased casserole dish (ovenproof). Flour top of dough and make traditional cross cut with knife. Bake at 375° for 50 minutes. Serve with butter and jam or marmalade.

*   *   *

Atlanta Falcons
6 Punter

JOHN W. JAMES, JR.

EIGHTEENTH-CENTURY BROWN BREAD

2 cups whole wheat flour
1 cup corn meal
2 teas. soda

1 teas. salt
2½ cups buttermilk
½ cup molasses

Combine dry ingredients in a large bowl; add buttermilk and molasses, stirring well. Spoon batter into a greased 2 pound coffee* can and cover with foil and tie securely with a string. Place can on rack in a 5-quart Dutch oven. Add enough hot water to cover lower half of the can. Bring water to a boil. Cover Dutch oven, and steam on medium heat four hours. Remove can from water and foil from top. Let stand 10 minutes. Turn bread out onto rack. Yield: 1 loaf.

*Baby formula is more common around our house than is coffee, so I use two empty one-pound cans of Similac powder. Bunnie.

MAXINE ISENBERG

N.F.L. Office—New York
Executive

FLOWER POT HERB BREAD

Wonderful gift idea for a housewarming or holidays. Two gifts in one. P.A.S.S.

5 clay pots—three or five inch. Soak clean pots in water at least one hour and cover drainage hole with small piece of foil. Grease sides and bottom. Put 1 cup warm milk and 1 cup warm water into large mixing bowl. Add two packages yeast and ¼ cup sugar, stirring until dissolved. Add ¼ cup melted shortening and 2½ to 2⅔ cups flour, save ½ cup flour for kneading. Knead for five minutes, then knead in 2 T. dried parsley, 1 teas. dried dill, 1 teas. dried tarragon and 2 teas. chopped onion. Knead until evenly distributed and let dough rise until double in bulk. Divide dough into five round balls. Let rise to double its size in flower pots and bake at 375° for 35 minutes. Serve in the pots at the table. DO NOT use glazed pots as they contain lead in the glaze.

• • •

DICK BUTKUS

Chicago Bears
51 Defensive Middle Linebacker
Hall of Fame

PUMPKIN BREAD

3 cups sugar	2 teas. baking soda
1 cup salad oil	½ teas. ground cloves
4 eggs, beaten	1 teas. ground cinnamon
2 cups cooked mashed pumpkin or	1 teas. ground nutmeg
1—16 oz. can pumpkin	1 teas. ground allspice
3½ cups flour	⅔ cup water
1 teas. baking powder	1 to 1½ cups chopped pecans
2 teas. salt	

Combine sugar, oil and eggs; beat until light and fluffy. Stir in pumpkin. Combine dry ingredients and stir into pumpkin mixture. Add water and nuts. Mix well. Spoon batter into 2 well greased 9¼x5¼x2¾ inch loaf pans. Bake at 350° for 65 to 75 minutes. Yields 2 loaves.

Seattle Seahawks
76 Offensive Right Tackle

STEVE AUGUST

HONEY BANANA BREAD

Here's one I know is everyone's old favorite, but I've made my own variations. Steve and I try to be more conscious of our sugar intake—plus with this recipe the bread comes out really rich, moist and has a very high volume. Susan.

SIFT: *1½ cups unbleached flour*

ADD: *2 T. baking powder*
                                            ¼ cup or less wheat germ
                                              ½ teas. baking soda
                                                 ½ teas. salt

BLEND UNTIL CREAMY: *½ cup butter*
                                               ⅔ cup honey
                                          ¾ teas. lemon rind
                                  ¼ cup dry buttermilk (instant)

BEAT IN: *2 beaten large eggs*
                                     1½ cups ripe mashed bananas
                                    (fold in chopped nuts if desired)

Let rest 5 minutes. Place batter in a greased loaf pan. Bake 350° for 1 hour.

• • •

Cincinnati Bengals
Coach—Defense

HENRY C. BULLOUGH
"HANK"

ZUCCHINI BREAD

This recipe freezes superbly and is so convenient to have on hand for entertaining.

Cream together: 3 eggs, 2¼ cups sugar, and 1 cup oil. Add: 2 cups peeled, grated zucchini (use a blender to grate), 3 teas. vanilla. Sift and add to creamed zucchini mixture: 3 cups flour, 1 teas. baking soda, 3 teas. cinnamon, and ¼ teas. baking powder. Mix well. Can add 1 cup chopped nuts or raisins. Grease and flour 2-3 loaf pans. Bake at 350° for 60-70 minutes.

TED MARCHIBRODA

NFL Alumni
Baltimore

BUCKWHEAT BREAKFAST CAKE
(Buckwheat bought at health store)

My favorite!

2½ or 3 cups buckwheat (groats)
1 qt. buttermilk
12 oz. cottage cheese (Sealtest) room temp.
¾ lb. unsalted butter
dash salt

Wash groats (buckwheat) put in strainer to drain and dry. Heat buttermilk, add butter, bring to boil. Add groats and salt. Cook 10—15 minutes, medium heat—no lid—stir often. Cook till liquid is gone. Cool. Put cottage cheese in when cool and before filling dough.

DOUGH: Pillsbury hot roll mix. Add 3 T. of sugar to flour. Follow rising directions on box. Roll out on floured board and put into pan 8x6 inches. Fill with groats and overlap ends of dough on top to completely cover. Bake 30 minutes at 325°, plus 10—15 minutes at 375° till brown. Delicious warm or sliced and heated. Keep refrigerated.

•   •   •

JACK GREGORY

Cleveland Browns
81 Defensive End

SOUTHERN CORN BREAD

Jack's favorite southern recipe. This is also a favorite of Dennis Harrison, Philadelphia Eagles, 68 Defensive End. Gwen.

2 cups self-rising corn meal
¼ cup bacon drippings
1¼ cups sweet milk (or 1½ cups buttermilk)
1 egg

Preheat oven to 450°. Blend ingredients thoroughly. Pour into heated iron skillet or corn stick pans. Bake about 15—20 minutes.

144—Souper Bowl of Recipes

Dallas Cowboys
80 Wide Receiver

TONY HILL

MEXICAN CORN BREAD

CORNMEAL MIXTURE:

1 cup yellow corn meal
1 can cream style corn
2 eggs
1 teas. salt
1 teas. baking soda
2 med. onions, chopped
2 jalp. hot peppers, chopped
1 cup buttermilk
3 parts of garlic, diced

MEAT MIXTURE:

2 lg. onions, chopped
2 jalp. peppers, diced
1 pkg. taco seasoning
1 lb. ground beef
3 parts garlic, diced
1 med. green pepper, diced
salt to taste
1 cup water

Mix together the cornmeal mixture. Cook meat mixture 10—15 minutes on stove top. Drain oil into cornmeal mixture. In skillet put half of cornbread mixture and add all of meat mixture. Top with grated cheese (2 cups). Add remaining cornmeal mixture. Top with paprika. Bake at 350° for 1 hour. Serve hot as a main dish. Make a tossed salad and you will have a complete meal.

•   •   •

Alumni
Buffalo Bills
15 Quarterback

**JACK KEMP
U.S. CONGRESSMAN**

SWEET MEXICAN CORNBREAD

1 cup margarine
1 cup sugar
1 can chopped green chiles (4 oz.)
1—16 oz. can creamed corn
4 teas. baking powder
½ cup shredded jack cheese
½ cup shredded cheddar cheese
1 cup flour
1 cup cornmeal
¼ teas. salt

Cream margarine and sugar. Add all other ingredients and pour into a greased 8x12x2 pan. Bake at 300° for 1 hour. Serves 10.

MARK D. MOSELEY

Washington Redskins
3 Place Kicker

CORN FRITTERS

Love those corn fritters!

>   1 cup pancake mix
>   ¼ cup milk
>   1 egg
>   1 can drained whole kernel corn
>   sugar to taste

Drop by spoon into oil. Fry in enough oil to deep fry just til golden brown. Serve hot with syrup.

*   *   *

GINO MARCHETTI

Hall of Fame
Baltimore Colts
89 Defensive End

POLENTA

>   4 cups water
>   2 teas. salt
>   1 cup polenta or white or yellow cornmeal
>   (waterground variety is best)

Bring the water and salt to a rolling boil using the top part of a double boiler over direct heat. Add the cornmeal in a slow stream, stirring constantly with a whisk. Cook until it begins to thicken, then place the pan over the bottom part of the double boiler which holds boiling water. Cook for 40—50 minutes, stirring from time to time. Wet the inside of a 9x5 loaf pan. Shake the excess water out. Spread the hot polenta in the loaf pan, smoothing the top to an even surface. Refrigerate until cold. To serve, slice the polenta ¼ inch to ½ inch thick. Saute on both sides in butter until golden brown. Or deep fry the slices at 375° until golden brown. Can also be served with a meat sauce.

Alumni
New York Giants 1935 & 1936
Offense & Defense

CHARLES TOD GOODWIN

GRIDIRON FRENCH TOAST

¾ lb. sausage, loose
4 slices of day-old bread
2 large eggs, well beaten
¼ cup milk

1 T. honey
1/8 teas. salt
1 small piece of sharp cheese

Cut football shape oval diagonally in bread slices. Save oval of bread for flag. Form loose sausage into balls with palms of hands. Take fingers and shape into footballs. Fry in skillet. Keep turning and pressing to retain its shape until browned. Pour off grease, add small amount of hot water. Cook until done. Place sausage in oval holes of French toast. Insert a stick or straw in bread oval for flag. Place flag stick in corner of French toast. Use soft cheese to hold flag in position.

•   •   •

Oakland Raiders
76 Nose Guard Defense

MIKE McCOY

BANANA ORANGE MUFFINS

1½ cups all purpose flour
½ cup sugar
3 teas. baking powder
¼ teas. salt
1 cup wheat germ

1 cup mashed banana
(about 2 med. bananas)
½ cup orange juice
¼ cup cooking oil
2 eggs

Mix flour, sugar, baking powder and salt. Stir in wheat germ; make well in center. In separate bowl combine banana, juice, oil and eggs. Pour into dry ingredients and stir until moistened. Fill muffin cups ⅔ full. Bake at 400° for 20—25 minutes. Makes 18.

AMOS MARTIN

Seattle Seahawks
50 Linebacker

BRAN MUFFINS

1—15 oz. pkg. raisin bran cereal
1 qt. buttermilk
4 eggs
1 cup salad oil
3 cups sugar
5 cups all purpose flour
2 teas. salt
2 teas. baking soda

Mix all ingredients well. Fill muffin cups ½ full and bake 25 minutes at 400°. Batter will keep in covered container 6 weeks in refrigerator. Great with any meal!

* * *

RONALD SINGLETON

San Francisco 49ers
67 Offensive Tackle

LOUISIANA YAM NUT MUFFINS

1¾ cups sifted all-purpose flour
1 teas. salt
2 T. brown sugar
3 teas. baking powder
½ cup chopped walnuts
2 eggs, well beaten

¾ cup milk
¼ cup melted butter
1¼ cups mashed cooked yams,
fresh or canned
cinnamon
sugar

Sift flour, salt, brown sugar and baking powder together. Add walnuts and mix well. Combine eggs, milk, yams and butter; mix well. Fill greased muffin pans ⅔ full. Sprinkle lightly with cinnamon and sugar. Bake in hot oven at 425° for 35—40 minutes or until done. Makes 12—2-inch muffins.

148—Souper Bowl of Recipes

Seattle Seahawks
87 Tight End

RON HOWARD

CINNAMON ROLLS

1 cup cool water
1/3 cup sour milk
1 T. dry yeast

2 T. honey
2 eggs
1 1/2 cups flour, whole wheat or white

Scald milk, add to water in large bowl. Check to make sure it's lukewarm, sprinkle yeast over and stir to dissolve. Stir in honey. Beat eggs in a separate bowl, then add to yeast mixture. Beat in flour. Cover bowl and let rise 1/2 — 1 hour. After rising, sprinkle 3 T. oil or melted butter over dough and 1 teas. salt. Fold into dough. Add another 2 — 2 1/2 cups sifted flour. Mix, then turn out on floured board. Knead 10 minutes adding more flour in as necessary, when it gets too sticky. Wash bowl, pour a little oil in the bottom, put the dough in and turn it over so the top is oiled. Cover and let rise until doubled, about 1 hour. Punch down, shape into ball. Let it rest 5 minutes. Butter a piece of waxed paper 15 inches long. Put the dough in the middle, roll out to a rectangle the same size as the paper. Dot with butter, brown sugar, cinnamon, and raisins. Roll up, cut into 1 inch pieces. Place them on greased cookie sheet or a couple of cake pans. Let rise 20 minutes. Bake at 375° for 20 minutes. Cool, glaze with powdered sugar and milk frosting.

* * *

St. Louis Cardinals
44 Defensive Back Special Teams

ROLAND B. WOOLSEY

CRESCENT DINNER ROLLS

4 1/2 cups flour
1 pkg. dry yeast
1 1/4 cup scalded milk
1/2 cup sugar

1/4 cup butter
1 teas. salt
2 eggs

Scald milk, add butter, sugar, and salt. Cool to lukewarm. Add yeast. Beat eggs and add to liquid. Add 1 1/3 cups flour and beat for 1 minute. Gradually add flour to stiffen dough. Turn out on floured surface and knead. Keep soft and easy to handle! Put in large bowl, let rise two hours. Punch down, let rise again 1 hour. Roll out and cut into triangles; roll individual triangles, starting at large end. Brush with melted butter. Bake 12 minutes at 400°.

RICHARD SZYMANSKI

Baltimore Colts
General Manager—V.P.

EASY REFRIGERATOR ROLLS

2 pkg. active dry yeast
2 cups warm water (110°)
½ cup sugar
2 teas. salt
6½ to 7 cups sifted flour
1 egg
¼ cup Wesson oil

Dissolve yeast in water. Add sugar, salt and about half the flour. Beat 2 minutes. Add egg and shortening. Gradually beat in remaining flour until smooth. Cover with damp cloth. Punch down occasionally, as dough rises in refrigerator. About 2 hours before baking, cut off amount needed and return dough to refrigerator. Shape into rolls and place on greased baking sheet. Cover; let rise until light (1½ to 2 hours). Preheat oven to 400° and bake 12 to 15 minutes. Brush with melted butter. Dough may be kept several days in refrigerator.

* * *

JOE REED

Detroit Lions
14 Quarterback

HOMEMADE ROLLS

Heat together: 2 cups milk, ½ cup shortening, ½ cup sugar. Cool to lukewarm. Dissolve two packages of yeast in ¼ cup water. When milk mixture is cool, mix in yeast. Add: 5 cups unsifted all-purpose flour, 1 teas. baking powder, 1 teas. salt, ½ teas. soda. Mix all ingredients together and refrigerate for a few hours. Roll dough into balls and let rise two hours before baking at 375° for 10 minutes or until brown.

150—Souper Bowl of Recipes

Detroit Lions
82 Defensive End

KEN SANDERS

YEAST ROLLS

1 cup shortening
1/2 cup sugar
1 cup boiling water
2 pkgs. dry yeast

2 eggs
6 cups flour
1 cup cold water
1 teas. salt

Cut shortening into sugar. Add boiling water. Put yeast in cold water to dissolve. Beat eggs and add yeast to mixture. Add salt and 6 cups of flour, 2 cups at a time. Mix and let rise for 1 hour. Put in refrigerator. May be kept in refrigerator and used as needed. * Bake at 350° for 30 minutes or until done.

*Roll into balls, place in muffin tins, let rise at room temperture until double.

JOE REED

Detroit Lions
14 Quarterback

RECIPE FOR PRESERVING CHILDREN

Donated by Mrs. James Pagnini, mother of eight.

1 grass grown field
½ dozen children or more
several dogs (and puppies, if in season)
1 brook
pebbles

Into the field pour children and dogs, allowing to mix well. Pour brook over pebbles till slightly frothy. When children are nicely brown, cool in warm tub. When dry, serve with buttermilk and baked bread.

P.A.S.S.
the
Dessert

Official SBR

P.A.S.S. SBR

P.A.S.S. SBR

DAVID STALLS

Dallas Cowboys
65 Defensive Tackle

BUTTERBRICKLE BARS

These are so easy and so good!

    1½ cups brown sugar
    1½ cubes butter (sticks)
    2 eggs, beaten well
    stir in 1½ cups flour

Mix above and spread on ungreased cookie sheet. Bake first part until golden brown at 350°. Remove from oven and immediately top with broken up Hershey bars (*2 large, broken up*). Return to oven until chocolate is melted. Spread melted chocolate evenly over top. Cool and serve. For chewier bars refrigerate.

•   •   •

BOBBY BEATHARD

Washington Redskins
General Manager

CHEWY BRAN BARS

    2 T. butter or margarine
    ¼ cup smooth peanut butter
    ½ cup honey
    2 teas. ground cinnamon
    ¼ teas. almond extract
    ¾ cup raisins (plump raisins
       in hot water to cover for 5
       minutes, then drain well)

    2 cups whole bran cereal
    ¼ cup brown sugar
       (firmly packed)
    1 cup chopped nuts
    1 teas. vanilla
    1/8 teas. salt

In a heavy 3 qt. or larger pan, combine butter, peanut butter, brown sugar and honey. Cook over low heat, stirring constantly, just till mixture begins to boil. Remove from heat. Add chopped nuts, cinnamon, vanilla, almond extract and salt; stir until blended. Stir in raisins and bran cereal, and mix until well coated. Turn bran mixture into a well-greased 8 or 9 inch square pan. With a buttered spatula, firmly press mixture into an even layer. Let cool until mixture begins to firm up, about 5 minutes. Cut into bars, and let cool thoroughly. Store in airtight container at room temperature. (Can also be frozen.) Makes 12 to 16 bars.

Baltimore Colts
52 Linebacker

TOM MacLEOD

GRANOLA

6 cups oatmeal
1 cup wheat germ
1/2 cup chopped nuts (walnuts, pecans, etc.)
1/2 cup sesame seeds
1/2 cup unsweetened coconut
2 cups raisins

1/2 cup safflower oil
3/4 cup honey
1/4 cup water
1 teas. vanilla

Mix all dry ingredients. Mix all wet ingredients. Mix wet to dry—mix well.
Bake in shallow cake pan until light brown. 325°—350° about 20 minutes.

*   *   *

Tampa Bay Buccaneers
77 Defensive End

BILL KOLLAR

LYNNE'S MINT BROWNIES

4 squares baking chocolate
1/2 lb. butter
2 cups sugar, granulated

1 1/2 cups flour
4 eggs
1 teas. baking powder

Melt chocolate and butter. Mix remaining ingredients together. Add the
chocolate/butter mixture to the flour mixture and add 2 teas. vanilla—mix.
Pour into greased 9x13 pan. Bake at 350°. Bake for 35—40 minutes. Allow
to cool on rack. Combine 4 T. butter, 3 cups powdered sugar, 3 T. milk and
2 teas. peppermint extract. Spread on top of brownies—put them in
refrigerator. Melt 2 squares baking chocolate and 2 T. butter. Dribble on
top of frosted brownies and smooth with finger. Refrigerate. (Cut into small
pieces as they are very rich.)

CHUCK CONNOR

Miami Dolphins
Director Player Personnel

PUMPKIN DESSERT SQUARES

18½ oz. pkg. yellow cake mix
½ cup melted butter or margarine
1 egg
1 lb. 14 oz. can pumpkin pie mix
1 teas. cinnamon

2 eggs
⅔ cup milk
¼ cup sugar
¼ cup butter or margarine

Reserve 1 cup cake mix for topping. Combine remaining cake mix, melted butter, and 1 egg; press into bottom of greased 13x9x2 inch baking pan. Combine pumpkin pie mix, 2 eggs and milk; beat until smooth. Pour over crust. Combine reserved cake mix, sugar, cinnamon, and butter; sprinkle over filling. Bake in 350° oven 55 to 60 minutes, or until knife inserted near center comes out clean. Serve warm or cold with whipped cream.

•   •   •

GEORGE HALAS, JR.

In Memory of
Chicago Bears
President

WALNUT SQUARES

1 cup flour
1 stick butter
1½ cups brown sugar
scant teas. salt

¼ teas. baking powder
2 eggs
1 teas. vanilla
1 cup chopped walnuts

Cream butter and flour. Spread in square baking pan and brown for 20 minutes at 325° or until very lightly browned. While that's browning, blend remaining ingredients. After well blended, pour mixture over cooled flour and butter mixture and bake in 350° oven for 40 minutes. After cooled, spread with thin layer of butter-cream frosting. When cooled cut in 1 inch squares. Should be chewy.

154—Souper Bowl of Recipes

Miami Dolphins
41 Defensive Back   NORRIS THOMAS

SOUTHERN COCOON

¼ lb. butter
2 T. cold water
2 cups chopped nuts
4 teas. sugar
2 cups sifted flour

Cream butter and sugar. Add flour and nuts. Roll into balls. Bake in slow oven at 350° for 40—60 minutes. Roll in powdered sugar.

•   •   •

Chicago Bears
71 Defensive End and Tackle   ROGER STILLWELL

"THE SPLURGE"

For real sweet tooths Roger and I love what we call "The Splurge!" We call it this because we allow ourselves to splurge on them only once or twice or three times a year! What you need...or don't need is:

2 sticks butter or margarine
1⅔ cups crushed graham crackers
6 oz. pkg. butterscotch chips
6 oz. pkg. chocolate chips
small can coconut
1 can Eagle brand milk
1 cup crushed nuts

Melt butter in 13x9 pan. Add ingredients as shown in order above. Bake at 350° for 25—30 minutes. Cool and cut into bars.

ANTHONY DAVIS

Alumni
Los Angeles Rams
28 Halfback

ACTOR'S CARROT CAKE

DELICIOUS!

1 cup all-purpose flour	2/3 cup vegetable oil
1 teas. baking soda	1 cup sugar
1 teas. double-acting baking powder	2 beaten eggs
1½ teas. cinnamon	2½ cups finely grated carrots
½ teas. salt	1 cup chopped walnuts

Preheat oven to 325°. Sift flour before measuring. Resift with baking soda, baking powder, cinnamon and salt. Mix together and add flour, stirring well. Add: oil, sugar, eggs. Add and blend well: carrots and walnuts. Bake in a greased and floured 8 inch square pan about 30 minutes.

CREAM CHEESE FROSTING
(Makes about 1 cup)

Work ¾ cup confectioner's sugar and 8 oz. cream cheese until soft and fluffy. Add 1½ teas. grated lemon rind and 1 teas. vanilla.

* * *

GEORGE YOUNG

New York Giants
General Manager

AMBROSIA CAKE

1 cup butter	FILLING:
2½ cups powdered sugar	¾ cup sweet cream, whipped stiff
5 eggs	2 cups powdered sugar
1 cup milk	1 grated coconut
3 cups flour	1 grated orange rind
3 heaping teas. baking powder	juice of a med. orange
1 teas. fresh orange juice	

Mix as any other layer cake and bake in moderate oven for about ½ hour.

FILLING: Mix these ingredients to spreading consistency. Put some of the coconut in the filling and sprinkle the rest over the cake.

Hall of Fame
Detroit Lions
NFL Alumni

JOE SCHMIDT

BANANA SPLIT CAKE

9x12 pan.
1st layer: 2 cups graham cracker crumbs, 1 stick butter and ¼ cup sugar. Mix well in pan.
2nd layer: 1 pkg. dream whip, 1 pkg. instant vanilla pudding (small), 1½ cups   milk. Whip in large bowl till very stiff.
3rd layer: 4 or 5 bananas, sliced.
4th layer: 15½ oz. can crushed pineapple, drained.
5th layer: 1 large container cool whip.
6th layer: 1 cup chopped nuts.
7th layer: 1 cup maraschino cherries.
Let set in refrigerator 2 to 3 hours or overnight.

• • •

Cincinnati Bengals
55 Middle Linebacker

JIM LE CLAIR

CARROT PINEAPPLE CAKE

1½ cups flour	*⅔ cup oil*
1 cup sugar	*2 eggs*
1 teas. baking powder	*1 cup shredded raw carrots*
1 teas. baking soda	*½ cup crushed pineapple with syrup*
1 teas. ground cinnamon	*1 teas. vanilla*
½ teas. salt	

Mix dry ingredients. Add oil, eggs, carrots, pineapple and vanilla. Mix until all ingredients are moistened. Beat with mixer 2 minutes at medium speed. Pour into greased and floured 9x9x2 inch pan. Bake for 35 minutes at 350°.

FROSTING

Cream together 3 oz. cream cheese, softened, and 4 T. butter, softened. Beat in 1 teas. vanilla and a dash of salt. Gradually add 2½ cups sifted powdered sugar. Stir in ½ cup chopped pecans (optional).

J. SCOTT HUNTER

Atlanta Falcons
16 Quarterback

CHOCOLATE CAKE

All men love chocolate cake with vanilla ice cream. Right?

1 stick oleo	1 teas. cinnamon
½ cup Crisco oil	1 T. vanilla
4 T. cocoa	1 stick margarine
1 cup water	4 T. cocoa
½ cup buttermilk	6 T. milk
2 beaten eggs	1 box powdered sugar
1 teas. soda	1 teas. vanilla
2 cups flour	1 cup chopped nuts
2 cups sugar	

In saucepan cook: oleo, crisco oil, 4 T. cocoa and water. Bring to boil. Pour over 2 cups flour, 2 cups sugar (mixed). Mix buttermilk, eggs, soda, cinnamon, and vanilla. Mix with spoon and bake in large (10x15) pan at 350° about 25 minutes. 5 minutes before cake is done, bring to boil: 1 stick margarine, 4 T. cocoa and 6 T. milk. Add powdered sugar, 1 teas. vanilla, and nuts. Frost cake while hot. Refrigerate before cutting as the cake will be very moist and gooey! Makes 60 squares.

•   •   •

RAY CALLAHAN

Washington Redskins
Offense—Coach

COLA CAKE

2 cups sugar	½ cup cooking oil
2 cups plain flour	2 T. cocoa
½ cup butter	1 cup cola

Mix butter, oil, cocoa and cola in a pan and bring to a boil. Combine this mixture with dry ingredients (sugar and flour). Mix with a spoon not a mixer. Then add ½ cup buttermilk, 1 teas. soda and 1½ cups small marshmallows, 2 eggs, 1 teas. vanilla. Bake 45 minutes at 350° in greased 12x9x2 pan.
ICING: Bring to boil ½ cup butter, 2 T. cocoa, 6 T. cola. Remove from stove and add 1 box sifted powdered sugar, 1 teas. vanilla, 1 cup nuts. Spread over warm cake.

Green Bay Packers   **BART STARR**
15 Quarterback
Head Coach

COCONUT PECAN CAKE

1/2 cup margarine	1 teas. soda
1/2 cup shortening	1/2 teas. salt
2 cups sugar	1 cup buttermilk
5 eggs—separated	1 can (3 1/2 oz.) flaked coconut
1 teas. vanilla	1 cup chopped pecans
2 cups sifted all-purpose flour	

Cream margarine and shortening until light and fluffy. Add 1 1/2 cups sugar gradually; beat again until light and fluffy. Add egg yolks and vanilla; beat thoroughly. Add flour sifted with soda and salt in thirds alternately with buttermilk, beating until smooth after each addition. Turn batter into a 3 qt. mixing bowl. Mix egg whites until stiff but not dry; beat remaining 1/2 cup sugar in gradually. Fold egg whites into batter gently but thoroughly. Fold in coconut and pecans. Spread batter in 3 greased, wax paper-lined, and again greased 9-inch cake pans. Bake at 375° for about 25 minutes, or until brown. Fill and frost as you wish. We use a boiled icing with additional coconut. Whipped cream also would be good. 12—16 servings.

•   •   •

Alumni   **EARL MORRALL**
Miami Dolphins
15 Quarterback

EARL'S FAVORITE CAKE

Take 2 pkgs. butter pecan cake mix and add 1 pkg. butterscotch pudding powder (either instant or other). Follow directions on box of cake mix, adding pudding as you blend. Pour into lightly greased sheetcake pan or two 9x13 pans. Sprinkle 1 pkg. butterscotch morsels on top and bake as directed. Mmmm Mmmm Good!

DAVID LINDSTROM

Kansas City Chiefs
71 Defensive End

EDNA'S APPLE CAKE

4 cups diced apples (about 6)
1 cup granulated sugar
1 cup brown sugar
1/2 cup vegetable oil
2 eggs
1 teas. vanilla

2 cups flour
2 teas. soda
2 teas. cinnamon
1/2 teas. nutmeg
1/2 teas. salt
1/4 teas. cloves
2 cups nuts

Cream oil and sugar. Add eggs and vanilla. Sift dry ingredients and add to sugar mixture. Fold in apples with knife. Add nuts. Bake in greased 9x12 pan for 50 minutes at 350°.

•   •   •

DARNELL POWELL

New York Jets
20 Running Back

FRESH STRAWBERRY CAKE

1 white cake mix
1/2 box of strawberry jello dissolved
1/2 cup of Crisco cooking oil
1/2 pint of fresh strawberries, sliced
1 teas. vanilla flavoring
3 egg whites

ICING:
Confectioner's sugar
(1 1/2 boxes)
1 stick butter
1/2 pt. fresh strawberries,
sliced

You add your ingredients in the order listed. Blend the cake ingredients for about 4—5 minutes (electric blender). This cake is not perfect and will not have the same taste if it is not a 3-layer. The icing is very simple. Blend smoothly. It takes only 4 minutes to prepare. The only hint is the cake has to be absolutely cool before icing or the warmth will ruin the icing.

Baltimore Colts
79 Offensive Tackle

DON MORRISON

GERMAN OATMEAL CAKE

1½ cups boiling water
1 stick oleo
1 cup brown sugar
1 cup sugar
2 eggs
1 cup instant oatmeal

1½ cups flour
1 teas. soda
1 teas. cinnamon
1 teas. vanilla
¼ teas. salt

Pour boiling water over oatmeal and 1 stick oleo. Add remaining ingredients. Bake 45 minutes at 350°.
TOPPING:
1 stick oleo
1 cup brown sugar
¼ cup canned milk

3 oz. can coconut
1 teas. vanilla
1 cup coarsely chopped pecans

Mix and pour over cake. Put under broiler until melted and lightly browned.

●   ●   ●

Buffalo Bills
79 Offensive Guard-Tackle

ELBERT DRUNGO, JR.

HILLBILLY CAKE

1 cup water
1 cup sugar
1 cup raisins
1 stick butter

1 teas. cinnamon
1 teas. allspice or nutmeg
½ teas. salt

In a medium saucepan combine all of the above ingredients and cook for 1 minute. Bring to a boil and let it sit and cool. Then add 2 cups flour, 1 teas. soda. Bake until it is brown on top. Bake at 350° for 30 minutes. Bake in one long pan.
ICING:
⅔ cup brown sugar
⅓ cup butter
3 T. milk

Melt and pour over hot cake. Put cake under broiler until icing bubbles (about 10 seconds).

TOM PAGNA

Kansas City Chiefs
Asst. Coach—Offensive Backs

JEWISH APPLE CAKE

This cake is tasty and moist. A young grad student at Notre Dame made one for a special event. My wife and I savored it and borrowed the recipe.

3 cups flour
2½ cups sugar
1 cup oil
4 eggs, unbeaten
1 can pie sliced apples, drained
chopped walnuts

½ teas. salt
2½ teas. vanilla
3 teas. baking powder
⅓ cup orange juice
4 T. sugar
1 teas. cinnamon

Lightly grease and flour large angel food cake pan. Set oven at 325°. In bowl, beat together until smooth: flour, sugar, oil, eggs, salt, orange juice, vanilla and baking powder. Put layer of batter (½) in pan, add layer of apples, sprinkle with cinnamon-sugar mixture. Add chopped walnuts. Put remainder of batter in pan, add layer of apples, sprinkle with cinnamon-sugar mixture and rest of chopped walnuts. Bake in 325° oven for 2 hours. Cool in pan 20 minutes, remove and cool completely.

•   •   •

MARK KONCAR

Green Bay Packers
79 Offensive Tackle

KLINKER CAKE
(Serbian Fruit Cake)

3—4 cups flour
4 apples, cored, boiled, peeled
1 stick butter (¼ lb.)
1 cup pitted, chopped dates
1½ teas. cinnamon
1 teas. baking powder
1 cup chopped walnuts

4 eggs
⅔ cup sugar
1 cup raisins
½ teas. cloves
½ teas. nutmeg
¼ teas. salt

Boil apples in about a cup of water (peel, quarter and decore first). Mash the apples and add butter to melt. In mixing bowl, add all other ingredients except flour, then mix. Add apple and butter mixture from pan. Add flour a cup at a time. Blend well. Put in long loaf pan. Bake one hour at 375°—400°, depending on oven. At 375° cooking time may be slightly longer. Remove from oven and butter top of loaf. If desired, a light glaze may be added while cake is hot. (This is a good cake to make ahead of time and freeze.) Test for doneness with knife or toothpick. When done, cake will appear a dark, golden brown color.

LOUISIANA MUD CAKE

2 cups Imperial granulated sugar
1 cup (2 sticks) butter or margarine, melted
1½ cups all purpose flour
2 cups walnuts or pecans, chopped
1 (7 oz.) jar marshmallow cream
4 eggs
⅓ cup cocoa
1 teas. vanilla
1 cup shredded coconut

Combine eggs and Imperial granulated sugar in mixer and mix at high speed for 5 minutes. Combine melted butter or margarine, flour, cocoa, vanilla, coconut and nuts. Combine the two mixtures and mix well. Bake in greased and floured 13x9x2 pan in preheated 350° oven for 30 minutes or until cake tests done. For best results, bake on rack in middle of oven. Remove from oven and spread marshmallow cream over top of cake. Wait a few minutes, then frost while cake is still warm.

FLOODTIDE FROSTING

½ cup (1 stick) butter or margarine, melted
⅓ cup cocoa
1 teas. vanilla
2 cups walnuts or pecans, chopped
6 T. milk
1 lb. (4 cups) unsifted Imperial powdered sugar

Combine all ingredients and mix well with wire whisk. Spread carefully over marshmallow cream. (Note cake is very rich and filling, so it can be cut in small squares to feed a crowd.)

MEXICAN CHOCOLATE CAKE

1 stick margarine or butter
1/2 cup vegetable oil
2 squares unsweetened chocolate
1 cup water
1 teas. baking soda
1/2 cup sour milk (1 1/2 teas. vinegar in 1/2 cup measure;
    fill with milk)
2 eggs, beaten
1 teas. cinnamon
1 teas. vanilla
2 cups unsifted flour
2 cups sugar

Combine margarine, oil, chocolate, and water in saucepan. Heat until chocolate is melted. Combine flour, baking soda, sugar, milk, eggs, cinnamon and vanilla in large bowl. Then combine with first mixture. Pour into greased 12x18 pan. Bake 20—25 minutes at 350°, or until cake is done. Five minutes before cake is done, prepare:

ICING

1 stick margarine/butter
2 squares unsweetened chocolate
6 T. milk
1 lb. pkg. confectioner's sugar
1 teas. vanilla
1/2 cup chopped nuts

Combine margarine, chocolate, and milk in saucepan and heat until bubbles form around the edge. Remove from heat. Add confectioner's sugar, vanilla and nuts. Beat. Ice the cake while still warm.

Cleveland Browns
60 Linebacker

BOB BABICH

MOLDED CHOCOLATE ANGEL CAKE

12 oz. pkg. chocolate chips
12 oz. angel food cake
3½ pints whipping cream

3 eggs, separated
2 T. sugar

Bake angel food cake and let cool. Melt chocolate chips and sugar over water (double boiler). While melting: beat egg yolks, whites and 1½ pints of whipping cream—*all in separate bowls.* When chocolate is melted, add egg yolks and *stir quickly* —(it will become hard to stir, so muscle up). Immediately fold this chocolate mixture into the *stiffly* beaten egg whites. When thoroughly mixed, fold in 1½ pints of *whipped* cream. Break ½ of cake into bite size pieces and place in the bottom of an 8x12 pan. Be sure to use only ½ of the cake. Cover cake with ½ of chocolate mixture, then the rest of the angel food cake (broken up), then the rest of chocolate mixture. Cover with the other 1½ pints of *whipped* cream. Sprinkle with chopped chocolate chips. Chill overnight if possible.

*   *   *

Cleveland Browns
8 Quarterback and Punter

JOHNNY EVANS

MORAVIAN SUGAR CAKE

1 cup hot mashed potatoes
1 cup hot potato water
4 T. butter or ½ cup shortening or
    ¾ cup butter and shortening
7/8 cup granulated sugar
2 slightly beaten eggs

2 env. dry yeast, dissolved
in ½ cup lukewarm water
2 teas. salt
4—5 cups plain flour
butter, light brown sugar,
    cinnamon

Cook peeled potatoes in unsalted water. Drain. Reserve 1 cup cooking water. Mash potatoes adding nothing. Mix well 1 cup potatoes, reserved water, butter, sugar and salt. Cool to lukewarm. Add eggs and dissolved yeast. Stir in flour until dough resembles heavy muffin batter. Cover; let rise in warm place until doubled. Punch down; spread in five nine-inch greased layer pans or ungreased foil pans. Cover; let rise to top of pans. When risen, punch surface with holes, fill holes with bits of butter. Cover tops with light brown sugar and dust with cinnamon. Bake at 375° for 20 minutes or until light brown. These can be frozen until ready for use.

GARY CAMPBELL

Chicago Bears
59 Outside Linebacker

OLD FASHION OATMEAL CAKE

1½ cups boiling water
1 cup brown sugar
1 cup white sugar
½ cup shortening
1 cup oatmeal
2 eggs

1 teas. soda
1 teas. cinnamon
1 teas. allspice
1½ cup flour
½ teas. salt

Pour water over oatmeal and let stand for 10 minutes. Mix in other ingredients. Bake in 13x9x2 pan 30 minutes (be sure knife comes out clean but cake remains moist), at 350°.

TOPPING

1 stick butter
½ cup brown sugar
1 cup nuts (pecans,
    walnuts or almonds)

¼ cup cream
1 cup coconut
1 teas. vanilla

Melt butter and add ingredients. Put on cake when taken from oven. Broil until coconut turns crispy-light brown.

•   •   •

FRED DEAN

Washington Redskins
63 Offensive Guard

PIE CAKE DUMP

2 cans of peach pie filling
1 can sliced peaches
1 yellow cake mix

¼ cup butter
1 med. bag of cut pecans

Spread peach pie filling, sliced peaches and cake mix over greased 13x9 pan. Melt butter and pour over cake mix. Spread pecans over cake mix and bake at 350° until done.

HAROLD CARMICHAEL

PEACH UPSIDE DOWN CAKE

¼ cup butter, melted
⅔ cup light brown sugar
1 can (29 oz.) sliced peaches, well drained
1 pkg. (2-layer) yellow cake mix—pudding included in mix
1 pkg. (4-serving) Jell-o instant pudding—vanilla
4 eggs
1 cup (½ pt.) sour cream
¼ cup oil
½ teas. almond extract (opt.)

Combine butter and brown sugar. Pour into 13x9 pan. Arrange peaches in rows on sugar mixture. Combine remaining ingredients in mixer bowl. Blend, then beat at medium speed for 4 minutes. Spoon carefully over peaches. Bake 350° for 50 to 55 minutes or until cake springs back when lightly touched. Cool for 5 minutes. Invert onto serving platter and remove pan. Serve warm or cool with whipped topping if desired.

* * *

Hall of Fame
Philadelphia Eagles
60 Center Linebacker

CHUCK BEDNARIK

POPPYSEED CAKE

1 box white cake mix
1 can poppyseed
Put 2 whole eggs in cake mix and substitute water for milk
1/8 lb. butter
pinch of salt
1 teas. vanilla

Beat eggs to mix. Heat milk and can of poppyseed and butter. Don't boil, let cool. Add poppyseed mix to batter, then follow baking. Bake at 350° for 20 to 30 minutes.

JIM KENSIL

New York Jets
President

PISTACHIO CAKE

1 pkg. Duncan Hines butter cake mix
1/2 cup oil
4 eggs
1 cup sour cream
1 pkg. pistachio instant pudding (Royal or Jello)

Filling:
1/2 cup sugar
1 teas. cinnamon
1/2 cup chopped nuts (pecans)

Mix first 5 ingredients 5 minutes on medium speed—very thick mixture. Combine the filling ingredients. In a greased and floured bundt or angel food pan, layer from bottom to top: 1st, 1/2 of batter, 2nd, 1/2 of filling, 3rd rest of batter and 4th, rest of filling. Place cake in cold oven. Set oven at 350⁰ and bake 1 hour. Can freeze. Serves 12—15.

•   •   •

KEN ANDERSON

Cincinatti Bengals
14 Quarterback

PUMPKIN CAKE

4 eggs
2 cups sugar
1 cup salad oil
2 cups flour

2 teas. salt
2 teas. cinnamon
2 cans pumpkin

Mix. Put in greased and floured angel food cake pan. Bake at 350⁰ for 1 hour.

ICING

1/2 stick margarine
2 teas. vanilla

8 oz. pkg. Philadelphia cream cheese
1 box X confectionate sugar

New Orleans Saints
85 Tight End

HENRY CHILDS

RED VELVET CAKE

2½ cups cake flour
1½ cups sugar
1 teas. salt
1 teas. baking soda
2 teas. cocoa

2 cups Wesson oil
1 cup buttermilk
2 eggs
1 teas. vanilla
1 lg. bottle red food color

Mix all ingredients at one time except for flour, beat until velvet and then add flour. Beat until flour is thoroughly blended. Divid cake batter evenly into 3 greased and floured cake pans. Bake at 350° for 30—35 minutes.

FROSTING

8 oz. pkg. cream cheese
1 stick margarine

1 box confectioners sugar
1 cup ground pecans

Beat together cream cheese and margarine until smooth, gradually add sugar. Add pecans last.

* * *

Alumni
Philadelphia Eagles
18 Quarterback

ROMAN GABRIEL

ROMAN CARROT CAKE

1½ cups safflower oil
1 cup honey
3 eggs
2 grated carrots
3 cups whole wheat flour
1 T. baking powder
¾ teas. sea salt

1 T. cinnamon
¾ teas. nutmeg
1 T. vanilla
1 cup pineapple
½ cup milk
¾ cup of walnuts
1 cup raisins

Blend oil, honey and eggs. Use flour, salt, baking powder, cinnamon, nutmeg, raisins and walnuts in another bowl. Add to blended mixture and then add pineapple, carrots, milk and vanilla. Use 9x13 greased and floured pan at 375° for 25 minutes.

SAM BAUGH

Hall of Fame
Washington Redskins
33 Quarterback

SAD SACK CAKE

2 cups bisquick
1 box brown sugar
4 eggs
1 can coconut
1 cup pecans

Mix together and pour into loaf cake pan. Bake at 350° for approximately 25 to 30 minutes. Test center with a toothpick.

•   •   •

EDDIE L. LEWIS

San Francisco 49ers
22 Corner Back

SAUTERNE CAKE

¾ cup of sauterne wine
¾ cup of oil
small package of vanilla instant pudding
4 eggs (med.)
1 pkg. of yellow cake mix
1 T. of butter

Mix all ingredients together adding pudding last. Use bundt cake pan. Bake at 450° for 50 minutes.

GLAZE ICING

⅓ cup butter
⅓ cup sauterne wine
powdered sugar

Add powdered sugar as to desired thickness of glaze.

Seattle Seahawks
80 Wide Receiver

STEVE LARGENT

SCOTCH CHOCOLATE CAKE

2 cups flour
1 cup water
4 T. cocoa
2 eggs
1 teas. soda
pinch of salt

2 cups sugar
1/2 cup margarine or butter
1/2 cup shortening
1/2 cup buttermilk or sour milk
1 teas. vanilla

Mix flour and sugar. Bring water, margarine, shortening, and cocoa to a boil. Add to flour mixture. Stir in remaining ingredients. Pour into a greased 9x13 pan. Bake at 350° for 35 minutes.

ICING

1/2 cup margarine
2 T. cocoa
3 T. milk

2 cups powdered sugar
1 teas. vanilla

In a saucepan, bring margarine, cocoa, milk to a boil. Add sugar and vanilla. Pour on cake when taken from oven.

* * *

Seattle Seahawks
63 Offensive Tackle

NICK BEBOUT

SOUR CREAM POUND CAKE

1 cup soft butter or margarine
3 cups sugar
6 eggs
1/2 teas. salt

1/4 teas. soda
1 sour cream (11 oz.)
1 teas. vanilla
3 cups flour

Combine ingredients in order. Bake in tube pan, 350° for 1 hour and 20 minutes.

TOM GRAHAM

Buffalo Bills
55 Middle Linebacker

7 FLAVORS SOUTHERN POUND CAKE

6 eggs	1 teas. butter flavoring
3 cups flour	1 teas. rum flavoring
1/2 cup Crisco oil	1 teas. lemon flavoring
2 sticks butter	1 teas. orange flavoring
1/2 teas. baking powder	1 teas. vanilla flavoring
1 cup milk	1 teas. coconut flavoring
2¾ cups sugar	1 teas. pineapple flavoring

Mix together butter, oil and sugar. Add eggs one at a time. Add baking powder to flour. Add flour mixture alternating with milk. Add the 7 flavorings, mix well. Pour into greased and floured bundt pan, bake at 325° for 1¼ — 1½ hours.

GLAZE

1 cup sugar	1 teas. each of 7 flavorings
1/2 cup water	

Let dissolve slowly in sauce pan. Do not boil. Cool cake in pan 15 minutes. Pour glaze over top and bottom of cake.

•   •   •

EARNEST RHONE

Miami Dolphins
55 Linebacker

7-UP CAKE

6 eggs	1 teas. butter flavor
3 cups sugar	1 teas. salt
4 cups cake flour	1 lb. butter
¾ cups 7-up	

Cream butter in sugar until fluffy. Add remaining ingredients alternately in small amounts. Beat 3 minutes longer after all ingredients have been added. Grease lightly an angel food or bundt pan. Dust with fine cracker crumbs. Bake 1¼ to 1½ hours at 325°.

Dallas Cowboys
70 Right Offensive Tackle

RAYFIELD WRIGHT

STRAWBERRY TRIFLE

Yellow cake mix (baked as directed)
1 pkg. lg. frozen strawberries
additional fresh strawberries (in season)
1 pkg. instant vanilla pudding (mixed as directed)

Bake cake; cool. Layer—cake, puddings, strawberries—repeat. Top with whipped cream, sprinkle with slivered almonds. (Best to make 24 hours ahead of serving. If you do, top with whipped cream just before serving.)

* * *

Chicago Bears
85 Wide Receiver

STEVE SCHUBERT

SWEDISH COFFEE CAKE

2 cups milk
¾ cup sugar
2 teas. salt
2 heaping T. shortening

1 teas. cardamon, crushed
2 yeast cakes, crumbled
4 cups flour

Heat milk with shortening. Add sugar, salt and cardamon. Cool and add yeast and 4 cups flour. Cover and let rise until doubled (2 hours). Add 2 cups flour. Cover and let rise until double (1 hour). Braid; put in greased pans. Cover and let rise ¾ hour. Baste with water and sprinkle with sugar. Bake at 425° for 20 minutes. Makes 3.

CHARLES HALL

Cleveland Browns
59 Linebacker

TEXAS CARROT FRUIT CAKE

1 cup 8 oz. diced mixed fruit
1 cup 5 oz. chopped pitted dates
1 cup 5 oz. dark seedless raisins
1/4 cup brandy
2 cups granulated sugar
1 1/2 cups coarsely chopped pecans
3 cups sifted all purpose flour

4 eggs
1 T. baking powder
2 teas. cinnamon
2 teas. baking soda
1/4 teas. salt
3 cups finely grated carrots

Soak fruits in brandy overnight, drain. Combine sugar and oil. Beat in eggs one at a time. Sift together flour, baking powder, cinnamon, soda and salt, reserve 2 T. Gradually add flour mixture to sugar mixture; mix until smooth. Coat fruits with reserve flour mixture. Stir in fruits, carrots and nuts. Pour into prepared tube pan. Bake in 350° oven for 1 hour 10 minutes to 1 hour 20 minutes. Cool 20 minutes. Remove from pan. Cool on rack.

•   •   •

BILL CURRIER

Houston Oilers
20 Strong Safety

ALMOND BUTTER CRUNCH

1 cup butter
1 1/3 cup sugar (granulated)
1 T. lite corn syrup

3 T. water
1 cup chopped almonds
4—4 1/2 oz. milk chocolate bars

Melt butter in a heavy 2 qt. saucepan. Add sugar, syrup, water and cook until it reaches hard ball stage. Stir in the chopped nuts. Spread on a greased 13x9x2 pan. Cool. Turn out on waxed paper. Spread milk chocolate bars on the top and chill in the refrigerator until firm. Break into pieces.

New England Patriots
73 Offensive Guard

JOHN HANNAH

GERMAN CHOCOLATE FUDGE

3 whole bars German chocolate
12 oz. chocolate chips
1 lg. can evaporated milk
1 T. vanilla
4½ cups sugar
2 cups chopped nuts
2 T. butter
1 pt. marshmallow cream
pinch salt

Break all chocolate into big bowl. Set aside. Put into big pan: butter, sugar, vanilla, and milk. Boil exactly 6 minutes. Add marshmallow cream to chocolate. Pour butter mixture over chocolate and marshmallow cream and stir constantly until chocolate is dissolved. Add nuts—put into large unbuttered pan.

* * *

Dallas Cowboys
Assistant Coach

ERMAL ALLEN

KENTUCKY BOURBON BALLS

1 stick butter
1 lb. powdered sugar
½ cup chopped pecans
(soaked overnight in 6 T. whiskey)
5 squares unsweetened chocolate
¼ cup paraffin

Cream butter and sugar well, add whiskey with nuts. Shape into little balls. If mixture is too dry, add more whiskey. Chill in refrigerator. Melt chocolate and paraffin in top of double boiler. Dip bourbon balls in chocolate mixture. Place on wax paper to cool. Makes about 70 balls.

VINCE COSTELLO

Alumni
Cleveland Browns
New York Giants
Cincinnati Bengals
Miami Dolphins
Kansas City Chiefs
50 Linebacker

MICRO-WAVE FUDGE

1 box powdered sugar
1/2 cup cocoa
1 stick margarine

1/4 cup milk
1 T. vanilla
nuts

Blend sugar and cocoa together in glass pan until marbled. Make a cavity in the center. Add margarine and milk. Put in micro-wave for 2 minutes. Add vanilla. Stir all together. Add nuts. Refrigerate 1 hour or 20 minutes in freezer.

* * *

DOUG SUTHERLAND

Minnesota Vikings
69 Defensive Tackle

MICROWAVE PEANUT BRITTLE

1 cup raw peanuts
1 cup sugar
1/2 cup white corn syrup
1 teas. baking soda

1/8 teas. salt
1 teas. butter
1 teas. vanilla

Stir peanuts, sugar, syrup and salt together in 1½ qt. casserole and cook 7—8 minutes. stirring well after 4 minutes. Add butter and vanilla. Cook 1—2 minutes more, then add 1 teas. baking soda and stir until light and foamy. Pour onto lightly greased cookie sheet, cool, break into pieces.

St. Louis Cardinals
23 Weak Safety

KEN STONE

PEANUT BUTTER FUDGE

2 cups sugar
2 T. cocoa
1/2 cup milk
1 T. Karo syrup

1 teas. vanilla
pinch of salt
2 T. butter
2 heaping T. peanut butter

Cook sugar, cocoa, milk and Karo until candy is between soft and hard ball. (Use a candy thermometer or drop candy mixture in cup of tap water.) Remove from stove and place pot in sink of about 2 inches tap water. Add vanilla, salt, butter and peanut butter. Don't stir, until bottom of pot is cool to touch. Stir until almost hard and pour into platter.* Cool, cut into pieces. The trick is to judge when to stop cooking and when to stop stirring. You don't want it to be too runny or for it to harden in the pot.

*Grease sides of pot and platter with butter.

•   •   •

Miami Dolphins
63 Center

MARK DENNARD

CHOCOLATE CRINKLE COOKIES

unsweetened chocolate (melted),
4 (1 oz.) squares
1/2 cup salad oil
2 cups sugar
4 eggs

2 cups flour
2 teas. baking powder
1/2 teas. salt
1—1 1/2 cups powdered sugar

Combine chocolate, oil, and sugar. Add eggs one by one beating well after each addition. Sift flour, baking powder, and salt together and add to chocolate mixture. Chill dough thoroughly for 2—3 hours. Roll tablespoon amounts of dough into balls, then roll in powdered sugar, and again between palm of hands. Bake at 350° for approximately 15 minutes.

JOHN OUTLAW

Philadelphia Eagles
20 Defensive Back

APPLE SAUCE COOKIES

1 cup light brown sugar,
  firmly packed
1/4 cup butter, softened
  to room temperature
1 egg
2/3 cup apple sauce

2 1/2 cups buttermilk biscuit mix
1/4 cup flour
1 1/2 teas. cinnamon
1/4 teas. nutmeg
1 cup raisins
2/3 cup chopped nuts

Heat oven to 375°. In large mixing bowl, combine sugar, butter and eggs. Beat until smooth. Add remaining ingredients; stir well with wooden spoon to blend. Drop by rounded teaspoon, 2 inch apart onto ungreased cookie sheet. Bake 10—12 minutes until lightly browned. Immediately remove from cookie sheet onto cooling rack. Makes 4 dozen.

*   *   *

STEVE FREEMAN

Buffalo Bills
22 Safety

BOSTON DROP COOKIES

These cookies are good to serve at baby showers with pink and blue icing.

1 cup Crisco
1 1/2 cups sugar
4 eggs
3 cups flour

1 teas. baking powder
1 teas. salt
2 teas. vanilla

Preheat oven 350°. Mix sugar and Crisco til light and fluffy. These cookies depend on the air beaten in them so be sure and beat sufficiently. Beat in eggs one at a time. Sift flour, salt and baking powder. Stir in batter and mix til smooth. Stir in vanilla. Bake in preheated 350° for 8—10 minutes on greased cookie sheet. Drop by teaspoon. These cookies don't turn very brown. Make your favorite icing, color it, and top cookies when cooled. Yield 6 dozen.

Baltimore Colts
49 Punter

DAVID LEE

COWBOY COOKIES

1 cup shortening
1 cup white sugar
1 cup brown sugar
2 eggs
2 cups all purpose flour
1 teas. baking soda

1/2 teas. baking powder
1/2 teas. salt
2 cups oatmeal
1 teas. vanilla
1 small package chocolate chips

Combine shortening, sugars, eggs, and cream well. Add (sifted together) flour, soda, baking powder, and salt. Mix well. Add oatmeal, vanilla, and chocolate chips. Drop by teaspoon onto ungreased baking sheets. Bake 10—12 minutes at 350°.

*   *   *

Minnesota Vikings
48 Running Back

SAMMY JOHNSON

"HERMITS"

1 cup seedless raisins
1 cup chopped nuts
2¼ cups all-purpose flour
¼ teas. salt
½ teas. soda

1 teas. cinnamon
1/2 teas. nutmeg
1 cup sugar
1 cup butter or margarine, soft
3 eggs

Sift flour, measure, resift 4 times with next 4 ingredients. Cream butter until shiny, add sugar in 2 portions, creaming well. Add eggs one at a time, beating until fluffy after each. Add flour in 2 or 3 portions, mixing until smooth after each. Stir in raisins and nuts until well distributed. Drop 2 inches apart by heaping teaspoonfuls onto lightly greased baking sheet into neat mounds. Bake 10 minutes or until nicely browned at 400°. Remove at once from pan to rack to cool. Makes 3½ dozen.

JIM MYERS

Dallas Cowboys
Assistant Head Coach

OATMEAL COOKIES

2 cups brown sugar
1 1/2 cups flour
2 teas. baking powder
1/4 teas. salt
2 cups oats

1 1/2 cups nuts, pecans
1/2 cup raisins
2 eggs, beaten well
1 cup melted shortening
1 T. vinegar

Sift sugar, flour, baking powder and salt together. Add remaining ingredients and mix well. Make in round balls, not too large. Cook at 425°, 10 minutes.

•   •   •

DAVID LOGAN

Cleveland Browns
85 Wide Receiver

PECAN DREAMS

1 cup butter
2 cups flour
4 T. sugar
2 teas. vanilla
2 cups finely chopped pecans

Cream butter and sugar; add vanilla, flour and chopped pecans. Roll into little balls and place on ungreased cookie sheet. Bake 30 to 45 minutes (until light brown) in 300° oven. Roll in powdered sugar. Let cool and roll in powdered sugar again.

Alumni
Los Angeles Rams
98 Halfback—Safety
T.V. Sportscaster

TOM HARMON

POLISH BUTTER COOKIES

They are super cookies and wonderful for a "snack" with a glass of milk. Having a double-benefit (two great cooks) in my wife and her mother, it's amazing that I don't weigh three hundred pounds. However, I asked the cooks for something "different" for this book and they suggested the "Polish Butter Cookies". . .different because they use hard cooked egg yolks.

1 cup butter	2 cups sifted flour
¾ cup sugar	½ teas. salt
5 hard cooked egg yolks, mashed	1 egg, beaten
1 teas. milk	finely chopped nuts
cinnamon sugar	poppy seeds
1 teas. vanilla	

Cream butter and sugar. Add egg yolks and vanilla. Stir in flour mixed with salt. Chill dough until it is firm enough to roll. Set oven at 350°. Lightly grease cookie sheet. On a floured cloth roll out dough ¼ inch thick. Cut with small cutter. Place on cookie sheet 1 inch apart. Brush with egg mixed with milk. Sprinkle with nuts, cinnamon sugar and poppy seeds. Bake 10 minutes or until golden. Makes about 48.

• • •

New England Patriots
48 Safety

TIM FOX

PECAN REFRIGERATOR COOKIES

l lb. butter, softened	1 teas. cinnamon
1 lb. light brown sugar	1 teas. baking powder
2 eggs	1 teas. salt
2 teas. vanilla	1 lb. chopped pecans
4 cups flour	

Cream butter, brown sugar, eggs and vanilla. Add flour, cinnamon, baking powder and salt. Add pecans last. Chill dough two hours. Divide dough in 6 portions—shape into rolls 1¾ inches in diameter. Wrap rolls in foil and chill overnight. Slice ¼ inch thick. Bake on greased cookie sheet 375° oven for 10 minutes or until delicately browned. Makes 14 dozen cookies.

WILLIAM CLAY FORD

Detroit Lions
Owner

APPLE MOUSSE BRETONNE

A very high calorie dessert.

4—5 med. tart apples peeled, cored and sliced	4 egg yolks
½ cup apricot preserves	¾ cup sugar
½ teas. cinnamon	1 teas. cornstarch
¼ teas. freshly grated lemon rind	1½ cup milk, warmed
pinch of nutmeg	1 env. unflavored gelatin
1 cup whipping cream	1 teas. vanilla

Combine apples, preserves, cinnamon, lemon rind and nutmeg in large saucepan and cook over low heat until apples are very soft—stirring. Transfer mixture to puree. Place yolks, sugar, cornstarch in top of double boiler and whisk until smooth. Add warm milk. Place mixture over simmering water and cook until thoroughly heated and slightly thickened—about 20 minutes stirring frequently. Add gelatin and vanilla and whisk until gelatin dissolves—about 2 minutes. Put mixture into a large bowl until it just begins to set. Whip cream and fold into chilled mixture. Add apple puree and whisk gently to blend. Taste and add more cinnamon and nutmeg if needed. Pour into 6 cup mold and chill.

APRICOT SAUCE

1 cup apricot preserves	1 teas. grated lemon peel
2 T. lemon juice	⅓ cup apricot brandy
2 T. powdered sugar	

Combine all but brandy and cook until preserves have melted and sugar is melted. Add brandy, sieve and chill. Serves 6—8.

182—Souper Bowl of Recipes

STEWART O'DELL

APPLE DUMPLINGS

Syrup:
2 cups sugar
2 cups water
¼ teas. cinnamon
¼ teas. nutmeg
¼ cup butter

Dough:
2 cups flour
1 teas. salt
2 teas. baking powder
¾ cup shortening
½ cup milk

Roll dough ¼ inch thick. Add chopped apples (to cover dough). Roll. Cut 1½ inch slices. Place in baking dish. Pour syrup over and bake about 1 hour 350°–400°.

*Peaches or rhubarb may be substituted for apples.

•   •   •

San Diego Chargers
54 Linebacker

JIM LASLAVIC

MY MOTHER'S CROATION APPLE STRUDEL

Dough:
3 cups flour
½ teas. salt
½ cup shortening
1 slightly beaten egg
⅔ cup warm water
¾ cup margarine—melted to put on dough after it's rolled out.

Apples:
1 bag apples
slice thin
sugar to taste
add cinnamon

Combine flour, salt—shortening, like for pie dough—stir in warm water and egg. Stir well and then knead for about five minutes. Divide dough in half and let stand in warm place for 1 hour. Roll dough then stretch dough very thin. Add apples and roll up. Bake 375° for 15 minutes. Then 350° until brown. Good with any meal—great warm with ice cream!

DON McCAULEY

Baltimore Colts
23 Running Back

CHOCOLATE MOUSSE CAKE

Serves 12—15 or one sore, hungry running back after a losing game!

2 pkgs. German sweet chocolate
4½ T. confectioner's sugar
6 eggs, separated
pinch salt
1½ cups heavy cream, whipped
3 dozen lady fingers
½ cup heavy cream, whipped

Melt chocolate and sugar in top of double boiler. Set aside. Beat yolks in a very large bowl. Add chocolate to yolks and mix with rubber spatula. Add salt. Carefully fold in 1½ cup whipped cream. Beat egg whites until stiff and carefully fold into chocolate mixture. Be sure to wash beaters before beating egg whites since they will not fluff up if beaters are dirty. Gently fold in egg whites to chocolate mixture. Line a glass serving dish or souffle dish covering bottom and sides with lady fingers. Pour half of chocolate mousse mixture into bowl. Add another layer of lady fingers and top with remaining mixture. Decorate top with any remaining lady fingers. Chill several hours. Serve with whipped cream.

• • •

THOMAS R. NEWTON

New York Jets
44 Fullback

APPLE COBBLER

¾ cup sugar	1 cup flour
2 T. flour	1 teas. sugar
½ teas. cinnamon	1½ teas. baking powder
¼ teas. salt	½ teas. salt

Heat oven to 400°. Combine ¾ cup sugar, 2 T. flour, cinnamon, and ¼ teas. salt. Mix with 5 cups sliced apples. Dot with 1 T. butter. Cover with foil, bake 15 minutes. Sift flour 1 teas. sugar, baking powder, and ½ teas. salt. Cut in 3 T. shortening, stir in ½ cup milk. Drop by spoonfuls on hot apples. Bake uncovered 25—35 minutes. Makes six servings.

San Francisco 49ers   **SCOTT BULL**
19 Quarterback

EASY PEACH COBBLER

1 cup sugar
¾ cup flour and ½ teas. baking powder
1 stick butter
2 large cans sliced peaches, drained
  (save juice of one can)
milk to moisten
cinnamon

Mix together 1 cup of sugar, ¾ cup of flour and ½ teaspoon of baking powder. Add enough milk to make batter like pancake mix. Melt one stick of butter in casserole and pour batter on top of it. Spoon two large cans of peaches on top of batter. Pour juice from only one can over it. Sprinkle cinnamon on peaches. Cook at 350° for 1 hour.

•   •   •

Kansas City Chiefs   **TED McKNIGHT**
22 Fullback

CANADIAN SQUIRREL FOOD

½ cup soft butter   *½ teas. salt*
1 cup sugar   *1 egg*
1½ cups flour   *1 cup chopped nuts*
1 cup brown sugar   *1 teas. vanilla*
1 teas. baking powder

Mix butter and sugar. Add egg, slightly beaten. Spread thin on greased 9x13 pan. Add baking powder and salt. Then spread 1 cup chopped nuts on top. In a separate bowl: beat 2 egg whites stiff and add 1 teas. vanilla and 1 cup brown sugar. Now spread this mixture over nuts. Bake ½ hour at 325°.

RUBIN CARTER

Denver Broncos
68 Defensive Tackle

PEACH COBBLER

2 pie shells
1 can peaches, drained & cut in wedges
3 eggs
1 cup Carnation evaporated milk
1 T. vanilla flavor

1 T. cinnamon
1 T. nutmeg
1 cup sugar
½ stick butter

Beat eggs; pour into mixture of flavor, cinnamon, nutmeg, sugar and milk. Combine with peaches, mix well. Pour filling into baked pie shell. Cut slices of extra pie shell into strips of 8½ inches. Arrange 4 pastry strips 1 inch apart across filling and weave first cross-strip folding back every other strip going the other way. Combine weaving across strips in this manner until lattice type crossing is completed. Bake until brown at 300°. (Thaw at room temperature.)

* * *

DEWEY SELMON

Tampa Bay Buccaneers
61 Middle Linebacker

ESCALLOPED PINEAPPLE

1 large can chunk pineapple, drained
1 cup margarine
2 cups sugar
3 eggs
4 cups bread crumbs
milk to cover

Mix margarine, sugar and eggs together. Add cut-up pineapple, bread crumbs and stir. Pour into casserole dish. Make several large holes and pour milk in each hole and cover over top completely with milk. Bake at 350° for 45 minutes or until firm.

Cleveland Browns
Linebacker Coach

MARTY SCHOTTENHEIMER

FROZEN CHOCOLATE DESSERT

1 can evaporated milk
1 pkg. 10½ oz. miniature marshmallows
1 pkg. 6 oz. semi-sweet chocolate chips
½ cup butter or margarine
1 cup (3 oz.) shredded coconut
2 cups graham cracker crumbs
1 cup chopped nuts
½ gallon vanilla ice cream

Heat milk, marshmallows and chocolate until melted and cool. Melt butter and lightly brown coconut in butter. Remove from heat, add graham cracker crumbs and mix. Pat ¾ of this mixture on bottom of 9x13 pan. Cut ice cream in slices. Place a layer of ice cream on crust and pour ½ of the sauce over ice cream. Repeat layer of ice cream and sauce. Top with remaining crumbs mixed with nuts and freeze.

*   *   *

New England Patriots
14 Quarterback

STEVE GROGAN

FROZEN FRUIT SLUSH

This is a great summer dessert and a nutritious snack for any season. I like to freeze this in soft margarine tubs for individual snacks. Fills about 8 tubs. If you like quick and easy recipes, this one is perfect.

6 oz. can frozen lemonade
6 oz. can frozen orange juice
8 oz. can crushed pineapple
1 small bottle maraschino cherries cut in halves with juice
16 oz. carton sliced frozen strawberries
3 diced bananas
2½ cups water
1 cup sugar
½ teas. wild cherry flavoring (opt.)

(Can add rum to taste, if desired.) Partly thaw frozen ingredients. Combine all ingredients. Place in large bowl or individual serving dishes. Freeze. Remove from freezer about ½ hour before serving.

BOB LORD

New York Giants
Offensive Backfield Coach

GRAPENUT PUDDING

My favorite dessert since I was a little boy.

> *1 cup grapenuts*
> *dash salt*
> *2 oranges cut up small*
> *2 bananas (do the last thing)*
> *1 small bottle cherries (maraschino)*
> *½—¾ cup sugar*
> *½ pt. heavy cream*

Put grapenuts in bowl. Add oranges, cherries, and bananas all cut in small pieces. Add salt and sugar. Whip cream. Mix all together. Chill and serve.

•   •   •

BILL CURRY

Green Bay Packers
Alumni

TINY SOUTHERN PECAN TARTS

> *3 oz. pkg. cream cheese*
> *½ cup butter or margarine*
> *1 cup sifted all purpose flour*

Combine cream cheese and butter. Blend in flour. Chill one hour. Shape into 1 inch balls and press into tiny ungreased muffin tins.

FILLING:

> *1 egg*
> *¾ cup brown sugar*
> *1 T. butter or margarine, melted*
>
> *⅔ cup coarsely chopped pecans*
> *1 teas. vanilla*

Beat egg, add brown sugar, melted butter and vanilla. Mix well and stir in pecans. Pour into prepared shells and bake at 325° for 25 minutes. Cool before removing from pans. Yields about 20, quadruple the recipe to serve 40—50.

Alumni
Miami Dolphins
21 Safety

RICK VOLK

PINEAPPLE DESSERT

½ lb. vanilla wafers—ground
1 cup confectioners sugar
2 eggs
½ cup softened butter.

Put layer of vanilla wafers on bottom of 9x9 glass dish. Save a few to sprinkle on top of completed desert. Beat together sugar, eggs, and butter. (Beat together sugar and eggs first, then add butter.) Add vanilla and pinch of salt. Put layer of butter mixture on wafers. Whip 1 cup of heavy cream and fold in 1 cup of well-drained crushed pineapple. Spread this mixture over butter mixture. Sprinkle a few ground wafers on top. Place in refrigerator and chill overnight.

•   •   •

Pittsburgh Steelers
Offensive Line Coach

ROLLIE DOTSCH

PISTACHIO DREAM DESSERT

2 T. sugar
1 cup flour
1 stick of oleo
½ cup of finely chopped
    pecan walnuts
2½ cups cold milk

½ carton (12 oz.) cool whip
8 oz. pkg. softened cream cheese
⅓ cup powdered sugar
2 small pkgs. (3¾ oz.) instant
    pistachio pudding

Crust: Mix well sugar, flour oleo, and pecan walnuts. Press in 9x13 pan. Bake for 15 minutes in 350° oven, cool.

First layer: Beat together ½ carton cool whip, cream cheese, and powdered sugar and spread on top of crust.

Second layer: Mix pudding with milk. Pour on top of first layer and refrigerate about 4 hours.

Final step: Just before serving, top with remainder of cool whip and garnish with additional chopped nuts.

WADE PHILLIPS

Houston Oilers
Defensive Line Coach

PRALINE CHEESECAKE

1¼ cup crushed graham crackers
¼ cup sugar
1 cup packed brown sugar
5⅓ oz. can (⅔) evaporated milk
3 eggs
¼ cup chopped pecans, toasted
3 8 oz. pkgs. cream cheese, softened
2 T. all purpose flour
1½ teas. vanilla
1 cup pecan halves, toasted

In small mixing bowl, combine cracker crumbs, granulated sugar, chopped pecans. Stir in melted butter. Press over bottom and 1½ inches up sides of 9 inch spring form pan. Bake 350° for 10 minutes. Beat together cream cheese, 1 cup brown sugar, evaporated milk, flour and vanilla. Add eggs, beat just til blended. Pour into baked crust. 350° 50—55 minutes or till set. Cool in pan 30 minutes, loosen sides and remove rim from pan. Cool completely. Arrange nut halves atop cheesecake.

SAUCE

1 cup dark corn syrup
¼ cup cornstarch
2 T. brown sugar
1 teas. vanilla

Before serving, combine corn syrup, cornstarch, and brown sugar in small saucepan. Cook and stir till thickened and bubbly. Remove from heat, stir in vanilla. Cool slightly. To serve, spoon some of the warm sauce over the nuts on cheesecake. Pass remaining sauce. 12—16 servings.

Seattle Seahawks
16 Quarterback

STEVE MYER

SOPAIPILLAS

2 cups flour
2 teas. baking powder
2 T. shortening

1 teas. salt
1/2 cup water
oil for deep frying

Sift flour with baking powder and salt. Work in shortening and water. Mix into soft dough. Roll out into a thin rectangle on floured board and cut into diamonds. Heat oil in a skillet to 400°. Add a few sopaipillas. Push under oil a few times so they are puffy. Cook on both sides. Drain on paper towel. These are good with any Mexican food.

To eat: Punch hole in middle of Sopa's, add honey or whatever filling you like. Makes 20.

•   •   •

Atlanta Falcons
89 Wide Receiver

WALLACE FRANCIS

STRAWBERRY DELIGHT

1 pkg. frozen strawberries
small carton cottage cheese
small pkg. strawberry jello
large carton cool whip
large can crushed pineapple
1 cup chopped pecans

Prepare strawberry jello according to pkg. directions and stir in cottage cheese and cool whip. Strain juice of crushed pineapple. Stir in mixture. Stir into thawed strawberries. Stir in chopped pecans. Chill until set. (Several hours) Serves 6.

JAMES (DUCK) WHITE

Minnesota Vikings
72 Defensive Tackle

STRAWBERRY SHORTCAKE

1 qt. fresh strawberries
1 cup sugar
2 cups all purpose flour
2 T. sugar
3 teas. baking powder

1 teas. salt
1/3 cup shortening
1 cup milk
butter or margarine
light cream or sweetened
whipped cream

Slice strawberries. Sprinkle with 1 cup sugar and let stand 1 hour. Heat oven 450°. Grease round layer pan. Measure flour, 2 T. sugar, baking powder and salt into bowl. Cut in shortening thoroughly until mixture looks like meal. Stir in milk just until blended. Pat into pan. Bake 15 to 20 minutes or until golden brown. Split shortcake while warm. Spread with butter, fill and top with berries. Serve warm with cream.

•   •   •

JERRY MEYERS

Chicago Bears
74 Defensive End

CHEESE TORTE

2 1/2 cups flour
1/2 lb. butter, not too soft
1 teas. salt
2 pkgs. dry yeast
1/3 cup warm water

1 teas. sugar
4 egg yolks
2 8 oz. pkgs. cream cheese
1 cup sugar
1 T. vanilla

Cut butter into flour and salt. Mix together: yeast, water, and sugar. Add to yeast mixture: 4 well beaten egg yolks until well blended. Mix all ingredients into flour. Divide dough in half; set aside. Filling: cream cheese (room temperature), 1 cup sugar, and 1 T. vanilla. Mix with blender till fluffy. Roll out half of dough on floured board. Spread cheese filling. Cover with remaining half of dough. Brush top with some of the egg whites. Use a cookie sheet. Bake at 350°, 30—35 minutes. For variety use pineapple, apricot or strawberry in addition to the cheese filling.

New York Jets
89 Wide Receiver

BOBBY JONES

CHERRY TORTE

2 sticks margarine
2 cups flour
2 T. sugar

Filling:
1st bowl:
1 pkg. dream whip
½ cup milk
1 teas. vanilla
2nd bowl:
1 pkg. 8 oz. cream cheese, soft
1 cup confectioners sugar

Mix margarine, flour and sugar like pie dough. Pat onto cookie sheet. Bake 18—20 minutes at 350°. Beat 1st bowl together; beat 2nd bowl together. Blend above 2 bowls together. Pour filling onto cool pie shell and place in refrigerator. Chill 6—8 hours. Top with 1 or 2 cans prepared pie filling—cherry, blueberry, etc.

• • •

San Diego Chargers
82 Tight End

PAT CURRAN

CHOCOLATE CREAM TORTE

½ cup 2 T. butter
30 sq. graham crackers
¼ cup sugar
1 T. cinnamon

1 cup milk
1 lb. marshmallows
3 chocolate bars (Hershey)
1 pt. whipping cream

Crush graham crackers with a rolling pin. Pour into bowl. Add sugar, cinnamon, and melted butter. Pad the sides and bottom of a round 4 inch deep torte pan. Set aside. Melt milk, marshmallows, and chocolate bars together over low heat. Cool at room temperature. Whip cream and fold into marshmallow mixture. Pour into pan. Refrigerate 8 hours. Serve.

ANDY FARKAS

Alumni
Washington Redskins
Detroit Lions
44 Fullback

DOBOS TORTE

12 egg yolks
12 T. sugar
12 T. flour
12 egg whites

1 T. water
½ teas. baking powder
½ teas. vanilla
½ teas. salt

Beat egg yolks, add sugar and cream until lemon colored. Add flour, salt, vanilla, water and cream. Lastly, fold in stiffly beaten egg whites. For each layer, pour 4—5 T. of batter into round buttered cake pan and spread. Bake 12—15 minutes at 350º. Remove from pan while warm. Repeat till all batter is used. Yields about 10 layers.

FILLING

4 egg yolks
½ cup sugar

¾ lb. butter
½ lb. sweet Hershey chocolate, melted

Beat egg yolks with sugar until thick and lemon colored. Add butter and cooled melted chocolate. Spread filling between cooled layers (except for top layer) and sides. Brown and melt 4 T. granulated sugar (carmelize). Pour over top layer of torte and spread with spatula.

•   •   •

LAVERN "TORGY" TORGESON

Los Angeles Rams
Assistant Coach

GREEN (OR RED) JALAPENO JELLY

6 oz. Certo
6½ cups sugar

1 jar pickled jalapeno peppers
1½ cups cidar vinegar

Chop peppers. Bring cidar vinegar, sugar and peppers to boil, 12—15 minutes. Strain. Add Certo. Boil 1 minute. Add any coloring (green). Pour in small containers. Serve over cream cheese with crackers.

Seattle Seahawks
12 Quarterback

DALE ADKINS

YOGURT & JELLO DESSERT

Nice and light and oh so pretty — P.A.S.S.

Make up one small package of any flavor jello. Let set in fridge. Mix 1 pint of yogurt (type with fruit at bottom) with 9 ounces cool whip, and spread on top of set jello. Place fresh strawberries and sliced bananas on top. Make up one small package of jello, let set only ½ way, then pour it on top of the cool whip and yogurt — let set.

•   •   •

Chicago Bears
Vice-President

ED McCASKEY

OLD COUNTRY STRAWBERRY JAM

This is good because it calls for ½ the usual amount of sugar.

6 cups hulled strawberries
3 cups sugar

Put strawberries in a large heavy saucepan and mash. Cook over moderate heat until fairly thick, stirring frequently. Gradually add sugar; stir constantly over low heat until sugar is dissolved. Bring to boil and boil rapidly for 15 to 20 minutes, or until juice sheets from spoon, stirring occasionally to prevent sticking. Skim, and pour into hot sterilized jars. Seal. Makes four ½ pints.

HAROLD "RED" GRANGE

Hall of Fame
Chicago Bears
77 Halfback

CRANBERRY SHERBERT

When cranberries come on the market, I plan to freeze a few packages so that I can make this sherbert during the summer. It is just great for a luncheon with Chicken ala King in Patty shells. Can be placed in a lettuce cup instead of a dish—but it melts quite fast.

1 pkg. cranberries (1 lb.)
1½ cups water
2 cups sugar
juice of 2 oranges
grated rind of 1 orange
3 egg whites

Cook cranberries with water 10 minutes. Cool slightly then blend in blender (or put through sieve). Add sugar and cook another 7 minutes. Cool to room temperature. Add juice and grated orange rind. Fold in stiffly beaten egg whites. Pour into 2 ice cube trays and place in freezer. Stir once or twice after partially frozen. Freeze firmly. Serve in individual dishes as a side dish with chicken, turkey, etc. (Especially pretty served in a sherbert glass).

• • •

STEVE MOORE

Buffalo Bills
Special Assignments Coach

HOMEMADE STRAWBERRY ICE CREAM

5 eggs
3 cups sugar
4 boxes fresh strawberries
juice from 1 lemon

1 pt. cream
1 can evaporated milk
2 teas. vanilla
dash salt

Beat eggs and sugar in blender. Add strawberries that have been washed, stemmed and halved. Pour mixture into ice cream freezer and add remaining ingredients. Freeze until firm, about 20 minutes.

NEIL ARMSTRONG

HOME MADE ICE CREAM

6 eggs   2 cups sugar
1/2 pt. whipping cream   1 lg. can Carnation milk
1 qt. Half and Half cream   1 teas. vanilla

Whip eggs in a large bowl for several minutes with mixer at high speed. Add remaining ingredients and mix well. Then try one of these variations or make up your own.

Fresh Peach: 8—10 large, ripe peaches, peeled and mashed, add about another 1/2 cup sugar and the juice of a large lemon.
Strawberry: 2 boxes of frozen strawberries and juice or 2 qts. fresh strawberries mashed with 1/2 cup extra sugar or more.
Grape: 1 large can Welches frozen grape juice (or more if you like stronger grape flavor) and juice of a large lemon.

Any of these variations may be added to basic recipe and poured into can of ice cream freezer. Finish filling can with whole milk. Proceed according to your own freezer directions. Makes 1 gallon.

•   •   •

CLARK GAINES

CARRIBBEAN FUDGE PIE

1/4 cup butter   3/4 cup brown sugar
3 eggs   12 oz. pkg. chocolate chips
2 teas. coffee   1 teas. rum extract
1/4 cup flour   1 1/2 cup pecans

Cream butter with sugar. Beat in eggs, one at a time. Add melted chocolate chips, coffee, rum extract. Stir in flour and 1 cup nuts. Turn into pie shell. Top with remaining 1/2 cup nuts. Bake at 375° for 30 minutes. Cool and top with whipped cream and chocolate shavings.

JOHN MAURICE SANDERS
"DEAC"

Philadelphia Eagles
Free Safety

APPLE PIE

apples (McIntosh and Rome combined)
   enough to fill a 10 inch pan
pastry for double crust for 10 inch pie
1 cup sugar and 1 T. sugar
2 T. flour
7 T. butter

Peel and slice apples. Place apple cores and peels in 1 cup water and boil, cook down to ½ cup liquid. Line 10 inch pan with pastry. Combine sugar and flour. Pour ¼ cup of sugar mixture into pastry lined pan. Add sliced apples. Add the remaining sugar mixture. Pour ½ cup liquid (apple) to the pie. Sprinkle generously with cinnamon and dot 7 T. butter all over pie. Cover pie with 2nd pastry. Trim excess and flute edges. Prick crust with fork to allow air to escape. Bake pie 15 minutes at 450°. Lower heat to 325° and bake 30—40 minutes more. Cool.

•   •   •

CHARLES ROMES

Buffalo Bills
26 Defensive Back

CHERRY PIE

2 pie crusts
1 lg. pkg. cream cheese
3 cups confectioner sugar

2 pkgs. Dream Whip
1 can of cherry pie mix
nuts

Cream cream cheese and sugar well. Whip Dream Whip according to directions of the packages. Whip in cream cheese mixture. Press nuts in the bottom of 2 raw pie crusts. Cook or bake until pie crusts brown. (Do not overcook.) Let the crust cool. Pour the mixture into the crusts. Top with the cherry pie mix. Chill for at least 2 hours.

198—Souper Bowl of Recipes

OTTO GRAHAM

BANANA CREAM PIE

Of all the baking I have ever done for Otto, this is his favorite. Bev.

2/3 cup sugar
6 T. flour
1/2 cup cold milk
1 1/2 cups scalded milk
3 egg yolks, beaten

1/4 teas. salt
2 T. butter
1 teas. vanilla
9 inch baked pie shell

Mix sugar and flour; add cold milk and blend thoroughly. Stirring constantly, pour mixture into scalded milk set on top of double boiler. Stir and cook until thickened throughout. Cover and cook about 10 minutes. Stir 2 or 3 times to keep smooth. Blend a small quantity of the hot mixture with the beaten egg yolks. Combine with mixture in double boiler. Cook stirring constantly, 2 or 3 minutes to cook the egg. Remove from fire; add salt and butter. Cool slightly; add vanilla. Cool thoroughly. Pour into cooled, baked pie shell. Cover with meringue made of the 3 egg whites and bake at 350° for 10 to 18 minutes.

*   *   *

RALPH WILSON

CHESS PIE

1 rind of 1 lg. lemon
3 egg yolks
4 T. cream
strained juice of lemon

1/2 cup sugar
2 egg whites
1/2 cup melted butter
orange rind

Grind rind of 1 large lemon. Mix it with sugar. Add the well-beaten yolks of 3 eggs and well-beaten whites of 2 eggs. Mix together thoroughly. Add 4 T. cream, 1/2 cup melted butter and the strained juice of the lemon (stir in quickly). Add orange rind. Line 8—10 small tartlett pans with flaky pastry and half fill them with the mixture. Bake 30 minutes at 350° pre-heated.

GEORGE W. ROBERTS

Miami Dolphins
4 Punter

BLACK BOTTOM PIE

½ cup sugar	1 baked pie shell (deep dish or 10" pan)
1 T. cornstarch	1 T. gelatin (1 envelope)
2 cups milk, scalded	¼ cup cold water
4 beaten egg yolks	4 egg whites
6 oz. pkg. semisweet chocolate pieces	½ cup sugar
1 teas. vanilla	

Combine sugar and cornstarch, slowly add scalded milk to beaten egg yolks. Stir in sugar mixture. Cook in top of double boiler until custard coats a spoon. To 1¼ cup of the custard, add the chocolate pieces. Stir until chocolate is melted. Add vanilla. Pour in bottom of cooled, baked pie shell. Soften gelatin in water, add to remaining custard. Stir until dissolved. Chill until slightly thick. Beat egg whites, adding sugar gradually. Fold in gelatin-custard mixture. Spoon on top of chocolate layer and chill. Decorate top of pie with chocolate curls. Regrigerate.

* * *

ED RUTLEDGE

New York Giants
Talent Scout

SIMPLE LUXURY CHERRY PIE

1 pie shell, cooked	1 teas. vanilla
1 can cherry pie filling	½ teas. almond extract
1 can Bordens Eagle brand condensed milk	⅓ cup lemon juice
1 sm. container Handi-Whip	
(if frozen, let thaw)	

Combine Bordens milk, lemon juice, vanilla and almond extract. Stir until mixture thickens. Fold in Handi-Whip. Spoon into pie shell. Glaze with can of cherry pie filling. Chill 2—3 hours. Serves 6 pleased people.

New Orleans Saints
67 Offensive Tackle

JOHN WATSON

CHOCOLATE ANGEL PIE

1 cup flour
1 cup pecans
1 stick oleo
3 cups milk
1 sm. vanilla pudding

1 lg. cool whip
8 oz. cream cheese
1 cup powdered sugar
1 sm. instant chocolate pudding

Mix together flour, pecans (chopped) oleo (melted). Spread in a 9x13 pan and bake for 20 minutes at 325°. Mix together ½ cool whip, cream cheese (softened) powdered sugar. Pour this over first layer. Mix together 3 cups milk, vanilla pudding, chocolate pudding. Pour on top of second layer. Spread last ½ cool whip over 3rd layer, sprinkle pecans on top. Chill overnight!

* * *

New York Jets
52 Middle Linebacker

MIKE HENNIGAN

BISHOP'S CHOCOLATE PIE

1 sm. pkg. instant vanilla pudding
1 pt. milk
1 sm. pkg. instant chocolate pudding
1 pt. vanilla ice cream

Mix puddings with milk in mixer. Add 1 pt. vanilla ice cream. Mix well. To make crust: Mix til crumbly—1 cup flour, 1 stick oleo, soft, ¼ cup brown sugar, and ½ cup chopped pecans. Spread on cookie sheet and bake at 350° for 15 minutes. When sufficiently cool enough to handle crumble crust in 9x13 pan. Pat down. Pour pudding mix over crust and top with cool whip. Top with additional chopped nuts or shaved chocolate. Refrigerate.

HANK STRAM

Kansas City Chiefs
Former Coach
CBS Announcer

DERBY PIE

1 stick melted butter
1 cup sugar
1 cup corn syrup (white)
4 eggs
1 T. bourbon
½ cup chocolate chips
1 cup walnuts or pecans

Mix all of above. Pour into unbaked pie crust. Bake 45 minutes at 350°.

•   •   •

JIM TAYLOR

Hall of Fame
Green Bay Packers
31 Fullback

HEATH BAR PIE

Take graham cracker pie crust. Soften ½ gallon vanilla ice cream. Spread half of ice cream on crust, mash 4 Heath bars and spread crumbled bars over ice cream. Then spread the other half of softened ice cream over pie. Put in freezer until time to serve.

HEATH BAR SAUCE

½ stick oleo
1 cup sugar
4 Heath bars

1 cup Pet milk
2 T. white Karo

Combine oleo, sugar, milk and Karo and cook until mixture thickens. Put Heath bars into mixture. Serve sauce over pie before serving. Keep sauce at room temperature. (Crush Heath bars in a dish towel using a hammer.)

St. Louis Cardinals
53 Linebacker

STEVE NEILS

PEANUT ICE CREAM PIE

A terrific summer dessert.

9 inch graham cracker crust
1 qt. softened vanilla ice cream
½ cup plus 1 teas. corn syrup
⅓ cup creamy peanut butter
⅔ cup dry-roasted salt-free peanuts, chopped

Refrigerate graham cracker crust until well chilled. Place ½ of ice cream in crust. Combine corn syrup and peanut butter and drizzle half of this mixture over the ice cream. Sprinkle with half of the peanuts. Repeat with remaining ice cream, peanut butter, syrup and peanuts. Freeze until firm, at least 5 hours. Let stand at room temperature for five minutes before cutting to serve. Serves 7—8.

•   •   •

Alumni
Chicago Bears
7 End

ED SPRINKLE

PECAN PIE

¾ cup sugar
¾ cup dark corn syrup
¼ cup butter

3 eggs, beaten
1 cup pecans

Bring above to boil. To hot syrup add gradually 3 beaten eggs and 1 cup pecans. Cool. Pour cooled filling into unbaked shell and bake until firm.

STUART KING HILL

Houston Oilers
Offensive Coach

BUTTERMILK PECAN PIE

½ cup butter
2 cups sugar
2 teas. vanilla
3 eggs
3 T. flour

½ cup chopped pecans
¼ teas. salt
1 cup buttermilk
9 inch unbaked pie shell

Preheat oven to 300°. Cream butter and sugar until light and fluffy, adding ½ cup sugar at a time. Blend in vanilla. Add eggs, one at a time. Combine flour and salt; add small amount at a time. Add buttermilk. Sprinkle pecans in bottom of pie crust; pour custard mix over the pecans and bake one hour, thirty minutes at 300°. The top browns as it cooks. Best served at room temperature.

. . .

FORREST M. BLUE, JR.

Baltimore Colts
50 Center

FORREST PECAN PIE

Slightly beat 3 whole eggs. Add 1 cup sugar, 2 teas. flour, 1 cup white Karo syrup, ¼ teas. salt and 1 teas. vanilla. Line pie pan with pastry. Sprinkle 1 cup pecans in bottom of crust and add the above mixture. Then melt and slightly brown 4 teas. butter. Pour over pie and bake 15 minutes in oven at 400°. Reduce heat to 350° and bake about 30 minutes longer.

. . .

LUTHER BLUE, JR.

Detroit Lions
89 Wide Receiver

SOUTHERN PECAN PIE

1 stick butter
1 T. flour
½ cup sugar

1 cup pecans
2 eggs

Melt butter, add flour and stir until smooth. Add sugar and boil 3 minutes. Let cool then beat in eggs and pecans. Pour into pie crust and bake at 450° for 10 minutes then 35 minutes at 350°.

**New Orleans Saints
Linebacker Coach**

ED BEARD

SWEET POTATO PIE

Bobbie does the cooking and I do the eating!

1 lb. sweet potatoes mashed very fine (fresh or canned)
1½ cups sugar
1½ cups milk
¼ cup butter
3 eggs, well beaten
1 teas. vanilla
pinch salt

Mix thoroughly. Bake in uncooked pastry shell at 350° for 50—55 minutes or until firm. Top with whipped cream.

•　　•　　•

**Denver Broncos
Special Teams Coach**

MARV BRADEN

TEXAS BUTTERMILK PIE

A rich and delicious custard type pie. Cut in small pieces, a little goes a long way!!

½ cup butter
2 cups sugar
3 beaten eggs

3 rounded T. flour
1 cup buttermilk
1 teas. vanilla

Cream butter and sugar. Add eggs and flour. Add buttermilk and vanilla. Pour into 9 inch unbaked pie crust. Sprinkle with nutmeg. Bake at 350° for 40—50 minutes. (Use knife test in center to test for doneness.)

P.A.S.S.
the
Beverages

Official   P.A.S.S.   Sister Carol Ann

SBR

GERALD SMALL

Miami Dolphins
48 Cornerback

BACARDI PUNCH

I like this punch recipe for adults as a cool party drink.

> 46 oz. can Hawaiian Punch fruit juicy red
> 6 oz. can lemonade concentrate, undiluted
> 6 oz. can orange juice concentrate, undiluted
> 1 qt. bacardi light rum

Chill 2 hours, pour punch over large chunk of ice in a punch bowl and float fruit for that added touch.

•   •   •

RAY OLDHAM

Pittsburgh Steelers
25 Defensive Back

BERMUDA RUM SWIZZLE

> 2 oz. Barbados rum
> 1 oz. Jamaica rum
> ½ oz. apricot brandy

> juice of 2 lemons or limes
> ½ oz. falernum (or sugar)
> 2 dashes Angostura bitters

Mix in pitcher with crushed ice. Twirl with swizzle stick until frothing and strain into stem glasses. Serves 2.

•   •   •

DICK LANE
"NIGHT TRAIN"

Hall of Fame
Detroit Lions
81 Defensive Halfback

BANJE

> 1 part banana liquor
> 1 part creme-de-cocoa
> 1 part half and half milk

Stir in blender with crushed ice.

Los Angeles Rams
59 Outside Linebacker

BOB BRUDZINSKI

DAIQUIRI'S

1 sm. can limeade
1½ cans light rum

10 oz. strawberries (or)
4—5 bananas

Fill blender with ice. Mix with limeade and rum at high speed. Then add strawberries or bananas. Mix again—if too sour add confectioners sugar. You may also add a banana to strawberries. Serves 4.

* * *

Denver Broncos
36 Strong Safety

BILLY THOMPSON

FOOTBALL ANTIFREEZE

Guaranteed to keep you warm at temperatures below zero.

1½ oz. Grand Marnier
1 oz. Kahlua

1 cup coffee
whipped cream

Add Grand Marnier and Kahlua to coffee—top off with whipped cream. If you put in a thermos, use cream or dairy creamer instead of whipped cream.

* * *

Chicago Bears
23 Defensive Back

LEONARD WALTERSCHEID

FROZEN ORANGE SLUSH

4 bags of green tea
6 cups water
1½ cups sugar

12 oz. can frozen orange juice
12 oz. can frozen lemonade
1 cup vodka

Boil 6 cups water. Take out 4 cups and put in 4 bags of green tea. With the other 2 cups of water, mix 1½ cups sugar. Add 12 oz. can frozen orange juice and 12 oz. can frozen lemonade. Add 1 cup vodka. Freeze overnight. Serve with gingerale.

DERRICK GAFFNEY

New York Jets
81 Wide Receiver

HURRICANE

2 oz. Jero's Red Passion fruit cocktail mix
2 oz. fresh lemon juice
4 oz. dark rum (amber)
1 orange slice
1 maraschino cherry

Fill a hurricane glass with crushed ice and cocktail mix, lemon juice, and rum and decorate with orange slice and cherry.

•   •   •

DON WEISS

N.F.L. Office
New York

KAHULUA

This is less expensive than regular and just as good. Must use good, strong instant coffee.

4 cups sugar
4 cups water
1 vanilla bean cut end to end
4 T. instant Yuban coffee
1/5 (25 oz.) vodka

Boil sugar, water, and vanilla bean about 8 minutes. Add coffee. Cool and remove the bean. Add vodka. Strain. Bottle and age 30 days.

Miami Dolphins
87 Tight End

ANDRE TILLMAN

PUNCH

2 6 oz. cans frozen orange juice
2 6 oz. cans water
1 can apple juice
1 can peaches
1 can pineapple juice
1 can apricot nectar
3 or 4 bananas
2 16 oz. bottles 7-Up
1 qt. pineapple sherbert
1 pt. vanilla ice cream

Mix all ingredients, except ice cream, together in blender. Place ice cream in punch bowl. Pour mixture over ice cream and serve.

*   *   *

New York Jets
49 Cornerback—Safety

REGGIE GRANT

"TIMMIES ALASKAN"

A speciality of Bartender Tim of Bill's Meadowbrook Tavern, Hempstead, N.Y.

1½ oz. creme de coco
1½ oz. ameretta
6 oz. milk
½ cup crushed ice
whipped cream
decorative sugar
cherry

Mix well creme de coco, ameretta and milk. Add ice and shake. Pour into tall glass. Decorate with whipped cream, sugar and cherry. Have a good time!

WILL GRANT

Buffalo Bills
53 Center

MINT JULEP

1 teas. water
1 teas. sugar
6 mint leaves
crushed ice
1 sprig of mint
2 jiggers bourbon whiskey
confectioners sugar

To a 12 oz. julep cup or glass, which has been chilled in the freezer, add a syrup of water and sugar in which 6 mint leaves plucked from the stem have been bruised with a spoon and then removed. Fill the cup with crushed ice and add one jigger whiskey. Stir vigorously until the ice level has dropped an inch or more, then again fill the cup with ice and pour in the remaining jigger of bourbon. Stir again until frost has formed on the outside of the cup. Garnish with a sprig of mint dusted with confectioners sugar. Insert two short straws, and serve immediately. If not served immediately, place in the freezer for up to 25 minutes, then in the refrigerator until ready to serve, but do not add the sprig of mint until the last minute.

ALAPHABETICAL LISTING

HF* — Hall of Fame

INDEX

BEEF

C. CABBAGE

CAKES

CHILI

CHOWDER. . .(See Soups)

COOKIES

D. DESSERT

PIE

POTATO

PORK

SPINACH

SQUASH

STEW

ORDER BLANK

If you should win and have ordered one or more books with this order blank, we will award an extra $50.00 spending money for your trip. GOOD LUCK!

Yes, Northwoods, I realize what spendid gifts this book will make. Please send the following order to me at:

YOUR NAME_____

ADDRESS_____

_____
                                              Zip

_____ copies Trade Paperback @ $7.95, total _____

_____ copies Comb Binding @ $9.95,   total _____

_____ copies Collector's Cloth @ $15.00, total _____

            Sales Tax for Virginia residents, 4% _____

Shipping - .75 first book, .25 next 3 books,
.15 each book thereafter.   _____

Total Enclosed   _____

Rush order to us at:
                    NORTHWOODS PRESS
                        PO Box 249
                   Stafford, Virginia 22554

OFFICIAL *SOUPER BOWL OF RECIPES* CONTEST ENTRY BLANK

RULES: Predict the teams and the final score of the play off game. Entry blanks that do not include the correct teams will not be considered. Send this to Northwoods Press, PO Box 249, Stafford, Va. 22554.

Closest to actual score wins the trips—In the event of a tie, winners will be drawn by lot. There will be one winner from each conference.

Each Winner receives—for 2, air fare to Super Bowl and return, Friday evening meal—Friday lodging, 3 meals Saturday, Saturday lodging, 2 meals Sunday, free tickets, plus $100 spending money per couple.

DEADLINE is December 10, 1980—by Postmark.

• •

☐   I am a National Conference fan

☐   I am an American Conference fan

I predict teams and the final score will be

_____ _____pts.

_____ _____pts.

If noone has the correct score but does have the correct teams, the one with the closest score wins. In the event of a tie drawing will be by lot. Decision of judges will be final.

            There is no limit to the times you may enter. Facsimile entry blanks are not acceptable—only this official entry blank can be used.

Your Name:_____

_____

_____
                       Zip
                  Phone (   )_____